MERIDIAN PLUS

Student's Book 2

Jeremy Harmer

Including a section of communicative classwork and listening activities for extra language practice

Contents

Longman

Unit-by-unit language summary

Quest Productions

Carla Leone, the woman in the picture, is taking photographs of the Grand Canyon in Arizona. Carla is a photographer for *Quest Productions*. Seven years ago she worked for a big agency, but she didn't like it. Then she met Adrian Hutton.

Adrian and Carla did not want to work for big companies and six years ago they bought an office and started *Quest Productions*. There are four photographers in the company, Adrian and Carla, Rob Greenall, and the newest member of the team, Laura Scott.

All the employees at *Quest* have a meeting every Friday. Together they take all the important decisions because *Quest Productions* is a cooperative.

1

Look and listen. Ask and answer questions about the text using *what*, *when*, *why*, *how many* and *how often*.

Language focus

2

Make questions by adding a word or phrase from **A** to a phrase from **B**.

A	B
Where	do you go to English classes?
What	do you live?
When	are you wearing a sweater?
Why	do you do?
How many	does the class finish?
How often	students are there in the class?

3

Ask and answer about each other, like this:

How many brothers have you got?
—Two.
Why are you studying English?
—Because I like it.
How often do you go to the cinema?
—About once a month.

Writing

4

Write about someone in your class, like this:
.... is a .... lives in .... has (not) got .... and/or .... comes to English classes .... times a week. .... is learning English because ....

Three photographers

Quest

Name: Rob Greenall
Age: 26

Rob began taking photographs at the age of 16. He joined Quest Productions 4 years ago.

Last month - to the North Pole.

In 3 weeks' time - photos of ruins in Peru.

In a month's time - photos of dolphins.

Quest

Name: Carla Leone
Age: 31

Carla began taking photographs at the age of 20. She started Quest Productions with Adrian 6 years ago.

Last week - the Grand Canyon in Arizona.

In a month's time - photos of a power station.

In 2 weeks' time - photos of street markets.

Quest

Name: Adrian Hutton
Age: 40

Adrian began taking photographs at the age of 10. He started Quest Productions with Carla 6 years ago.

Last Saturday - the British Boxing Final.

In 2 days' time - photos of a parachute team.

In a week's time - photos of American football game.

Language focus

1

Ask and answer like this, using the verbs in the box.

When did Rob begin taking photographs?
—Ten years ago.
When did Adrian photograph the boxing final?
—Last Saturday.
When is Carla going to take photographs of a power station?
—In a month's time.

go	photograph
visit	photo
	take photographs

Read and write

2

Read this:

Rob Greenall is a photographer with *Quest Productions*. He began taking photographs ten years ago. Last month he went to the North Pole and in three weeks' time he's going to take photographs of historical ruins in Peru.

3

Write a similar paragraph about Carla Leone or Adrian Hutton.

4

Now write a paragraph about yourself, like this:

I am a .... I .... (two) years ago.
Last (week) I .... and in (a month's) time I'm going to ....

Casablanca

1

In the conversation Carla's answers to Adrian's questions are in the wrong order. What is the correct order?

What did you do yesterday evening?
What did you think of it?
Did you like Humphrey Bogart?
Did you go alone?
Who were you with?
What's she like?

3 Oh yes, he was fantastic! (A)
2 I thought it was very good. (B)
4 No, I didn't. (C)
6 She's very nice, I think. (D)
1 I went to 'Casablanca' at the Arts Cinema. (E)
5 Laura Scott. (F)

English in use:

Speaking

2

Make and answer questions with the following:

When/last see a film?
Where/see it?
Who/in it?
Did/like the film?
Who/with you?

Vocabulary work

3

Match the following professions and places by making sentences. Use a dictionary if necessary.

Example: A doctor usually works in a hospital.

Professions	
doctor	lion tamer
secretary	photographer
scientist	policeman
lawyer	actress
teacher	mechanic
cook	dentist

Places	
theatre	laboratory
surgery	kitchen
hospital	circus
court	classroom
garage	studio
office	police station

4

What is your profession? Where do you work?

Pronunciation

5

Listen to the cassette. Copy the words and underline the stressed part of the word. The first one is done for you.

photographer	doctor	teacher	policeman	actress
dentist	gardener	reporter	president	housewife
mechanic	secretary	scientist	lawyer	

6

What is the correct pronunciation of the name of your profession?

Reading

1

Read the following questions and answer them by reading the text.

1 Which film takes place in Nicaragua?
2 Which film is about a murder?
3 In which film does a photographer take a picture in a park?
4 In which film does a photographer take a picture of a dead man?

Two films about photography

Joanna Cassidy and Nick Nolte in 'Under Fire'

UNDER FIRE was released in 1982. It tells the story of a war photographer (played by Nick Nolte) and a reporter friend (Joanna Cassidy). They are both in Nicaragua during the Sandinista revolution. Nolte and Cassidy go to the revolutionaries' camp. Nolte is asked to take a photograph of the rebel leader, Rafael. But Rafael is dead. The rebels want Rafael to 'live again' so Nolte takes a photograph showing Rafael alive with his men.

Under Fire asks a question. Can a photographer take sides? Is his job to take part in events or only to watch them?

David Hemmings in 'Blow Up'

BLOW UP was made by the famous film director, Antonioni. It was released in 1969 and tells the story of a young photographer (played by David Hemmings). One day Hemmings takes a photograph in a London park. When he develops the film he sees a hand with a gun in his picture. Has his camera 'seen' a murder?

The answer is probably 'yes', and Hemmings tries to find out who the murderer was. But was the murder real? Can Hemmings believe his photograph? *Blow Up* examines the role of photography and its relationship with truth and reality.

Under Fire photograph © 1983 Under Fire Associates, A Greenberg Bros. Partnership. All Rights Reserved

2

Give the following information about each film, if possible.

1 Name
2 Date of release
3 Director
4 Actor/Actress

Remember

Present tenses

How often	do you go	to English classes?
Why	are you going	

Have got

How many	sisters cars	have I/you/we/they	got?
		has he/she	

Time questions with *when*

When	did	Rob	visit	the North Pole?
	is		going to visit	

A month ago.
In two weeks' time.

2 Parachute jump

INSTRUCTOR: How do you feel?
ADRIAN: I've never been so frightened in all my life!
INSTRUCTOR: Don't worry. It's going to be all right.
ADRIAN: Are you sure?
INSTRUCTOR: Yes! Parachuting is safe—and it's fun!
ADRIAN: Look, I've driven racing cars, I've sailed across the Atlantic, and I've even climbed mountains, but I've never made a parachute jump before and, now that we're up here, I don't really want to!
INSTRUCTOR: Why are you doing it then?
ADRIAN: Because I read an article about parachuting in a magazine.
INSTRUCTOR: We're over the jumping zone now. Get ready to jump. 5-4-3-2-1. Go!
ADRIAN: Help!

1

Look and listen. Answer the following questions with *yes* or *no*.

1 Has Adrian made a parachute jump before?
2 Is Adrian frightened?
3 Has Adrian ever driven fast cars?
4 Has Adrian ever climbed a mountain?

Language focus

2

Look at the pictures and say the words.

1 a famous person *met*

2 'I love you' *said*

3 an accident *seen*

4 a terrible nightmare *had*

3

Ask and answer about each other, like this:

> Have you ever had a terrible nightmare?
> —Yes, I have./No I haven't.

 Add some more questions.

Language focus

1

Study the information opposite.

1 This man is going to sail alone, not with a crew.

2 This woman is going to film on location, not in a studio.

3 These women are going to dance in a competition, not for fun.

4 These men are going to play for their country, not for local teams.

2

Ask and answer, like this:

> Why are the men nervous in picture 4?
> —They've never played for their country before, they've always played for local teams.

Read and write

3

Read the information opposite and complete the chart.

Cleaning your teeth

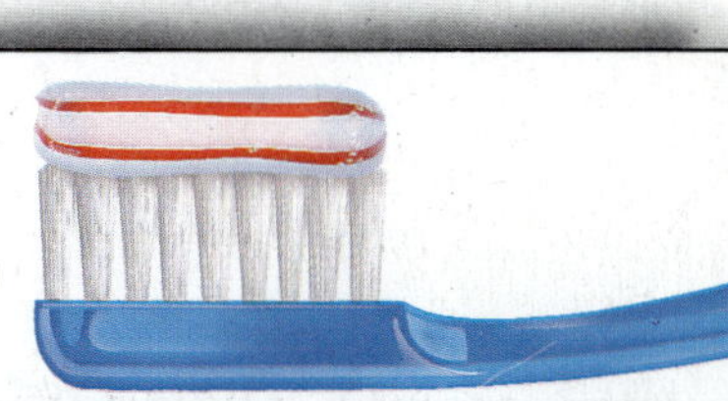

A recent survey has discovered some new facts about how often people clean their teeth.
90% of the people interviewed have always cleaned their teeth twice a day, 8% have always cleaned their teeth after every meal, but 2% have never cleaned their teeth at all.
15% of all the people questioned have never used toothpaste.

PERCENTAGES	ACTIVITIES
90%	....
8%	....
2%	....
15%	....

4

Look at the chart opposite about having baths and showers and write a similar paragraph.

PERCENTAGES	ACTIVITIES
80%	a shower every day
10%	a bath twice a week
10%	a bath once a week
9%	a shower – never

2 Terribly sorry

English in use: *Speaking*

1 Look and listen.

2 Have similar conversations, like this:

I'm (terribly) sorry. I'm afraid I've ....

Don't worry about it./It doesn't matter.

Here are some words to help you.

cup	glass	burn – burnt
juice	coffee	tear – torn
carpet	sofa	spill – spilt
book	key	lose – lost

Pronunciation

3 Listen to the cassette. You will hear some sentences. For each sentence say which word you hear, **a**, **b** or **c**.

1 **a** bury **b** ferry **c** very
2 **a** safe **b** save
3 **a** fans **b** vans **c** bans
4 **a** clubs **b** gloves
5 **a** habit **b** have it
6 **a** view **b** few

4 Say these phrases and sentences. Pay special attention to the pronunciation of *b*, *v* and *f*.

1 a very good club
2 very fat
3 I've had a bad foot.
4 I'm afraid I've broken a glass.
5 Brian didn't live in France.

Reading

1

Read the following questions and answer them by reading the text.

1 Why did Adrian make the jump?
2 What did Adrian do before the jump?
3 How does Adrian feel about parachuting now?

THE FIRST JUMP

Adrian Hutton, a photographer, recently made a parachute jump for the first time. He describes the experience to our reporter, Kay Feldon. Photograph by Helen Gray of the Cambridge Parachute Club.

I made my first parachute jump because I've always wanted to try it. I read an article about parachuting in a magazine and I liked the idea.

Before the jump I went to six practice classes. I was taught where to sit in the aeroplane, how to jump out, how to guide the parachute, and how to fall.

On the big day I was very nervous. The weather was cloudy, but the pilot thought it was all right, so two of us (the instructor and I) got into one of the aeroplanes with the pilot, and Helen Gray got into the other. (She wanted some parachuting photographs.) We took off and climbed to 1000 metres. I was really very frightened waiting for the big moment! Then the instructor told me to jump. I looked out of the open door and saw the ground below. It was the most terrifying moment of my life! I closed my eyes and jumped.

It was a great relief when the parachute opened! I looked up and saw the orange canopy. Below me was the landing area. It was really beautiful falling peacefully through the air. I landed well and waited for the instructor. Then we picked up our parachutes and went off to have a coffee and talk about the jump.

Parachuting is definitely more exciting than other things I have done before—like mountain climbing and sailing—and it's more fun, too. I'm going to make my second jump next week.

2

Answer the following questions.

1 What was the weather like on the day of the jump?
2 How many people were in Adrian's aeroplane?
3 What height did Adrian jump from?
4 What colour was his parachute?

Remember The present perfect

Have	I/you/we/they	ever	seen met watched	the President?
Has	he/she/it			

Yes, No,	I/you/we/they	have. haven't.
	she/he/it	has. hasn't.

They/You/We/I	have	always danced for fun.
She/He/It	has	

3 The Ascot Ballroom

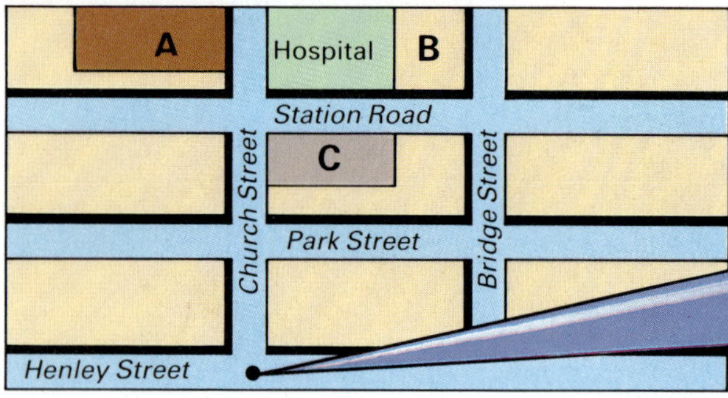

LAURA: Excuse me!
WOMAN: Yes?
LAURA: Can you tell me how to get to the Ascot Ballroom?
WOMAN: The Ascot Ballroom? Let me see ... er ... go down Church Street, take the second turning on the right and the ballroom's on your right, opposite the hospital.
LAURA: That's second right, opposite the hospital.
WOMAN: That's it.
LAURA: Thanks a lot!
WOMAN: Don't mention it.

1

Look and listen. Which is the Ascot Ballroom, A, B or C?

Language focus

2

Ask about these places, like this:

> What happens at ....?
> What can you buy at ....?

station	disco	theatre	post office
bank	restaurant	grocer's	newsagent's
butcher's	hotel	supermarket	chemist's
hospital	cinema	flower shop	

3

Study the map opposite.

4

You are standing at the spot marked with the red arrow. Ask and answer, like this:

> Can you tell me how to get to the chemist's?
> —Go down this street. Take the second turning on your right. It's on your left, next to the newsagent's.

5

Ask and answer about places in your area in the same way. Say exactly where you are first.

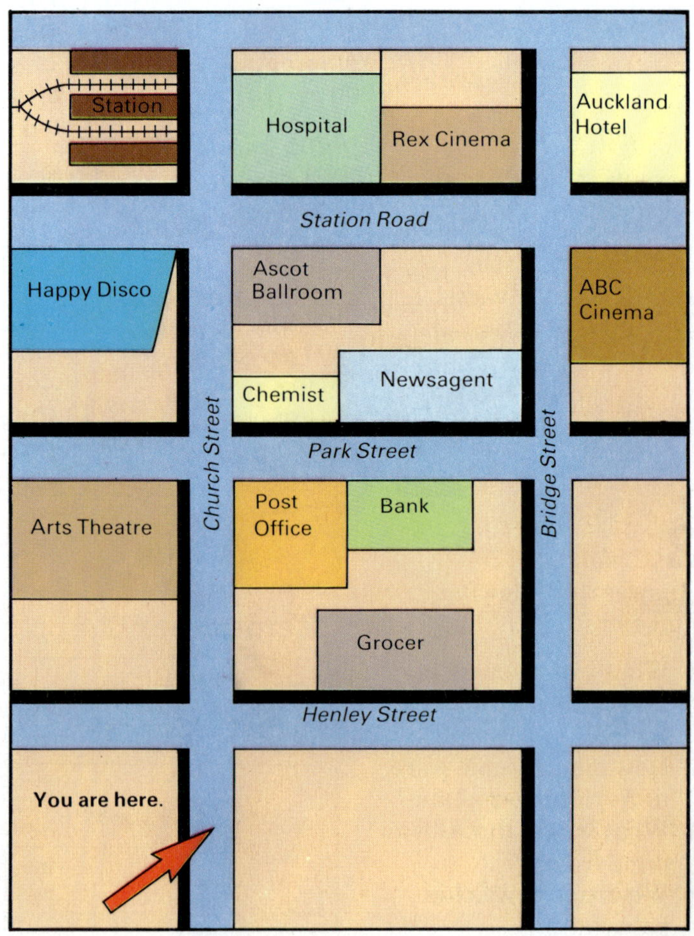

Language focus

1

Match the phrases in the two columns and write the instructions.
Use a dictionary if necessary.

taking a photograph	
press	1 the viewfinder
look through	2 the lens
wind on	3 the button
focus	4 the film

using a payphone	
dial	1 the receiver
put in	2 the correct money
wait for	3 the dialling tone
lift	4 the number

using a photocopier	
select	1 the cover
press	2 the paper face down on the glass
lift	3 the number of copies
put	4 the green button

2

Ask and answer, like this:

> Can you tell me how to use this payphone?
> —Yes. First lift the receiver and put in the correct money. Then wait for the dialling tone and dial the number.

Read and write

3

Where do these words go on the card opposite?

switch off
put in
programme
take out

4

Write instructions for another machine that you are familiar with, e.g. tumble drier, food mixer, coffee machine.

How to use this washing machine

1 Select the right .... and put in your washing.

2 .... two 50p coins and start the machine.

3 At the end of the programme .... the machine and .... the washing.

TELEPHONE MESSAGES

TO: *Carla*
DATE: *30/11*
TIME: *1615 hrs*
FROM: *Alan Sheerness, Technical Manager, Dinorwig Power Station*

You can go to Dinorwig on Monday or Tuesday next week. The director of the power station is going to be in Japan, but Mr Sheerness will be there. You can travel to Bangor by train or coach and they will meet you at the railway station – or the bus station — and take you to Dinorwig.
Please ring and confirm the date and say how you are going to travel.

MESSAGE TAKEN BY: *Laura*

English in use: *Writing*

1

Answer these questions.

1 Who rang Carla?
2 What is Carla going to visit?
3 Where is the director going to be next week?
4 Where is Alan Sheerness going to be next week?
5 How can Carla get to Dinorwig?
6 Which railway or bus station is Carla going to arrive at?

2

Join the pairs of sentences with *or*, *and*, or *but*.

1 I've ridden a bicycle.
I've never ridden a horse.
2 I often play tennis.
I always enjoy it.
3 I've heard of Steven Spielberg.
I've seen some of his films.
4 He didn't like the hotel.
He didn't enjoy his holiday.
5 Is she going to arrive today?
Is she going to arrive tomorrow?

3

In pairs, practise giving and taking telephone messages. One student (**A**) rings up and leaves a message. The other student (**B**) writes the message down. **A** is going to visit someone who is not in the office and leaves a message with **B** about date and time of arrival, etc. Remember to use *or*, *and*, and *but* where appropriate.

TELEPHONE MESSAGES

TO:
DATE:
TIME:
FROM:

Vocabulary work

4

Look at the pictures. Match the words with the numbers.

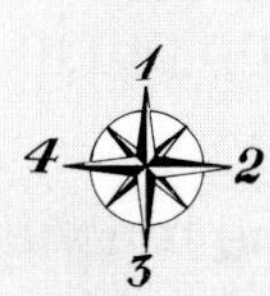

top	bottom	east
right	left	west
north	middle	south

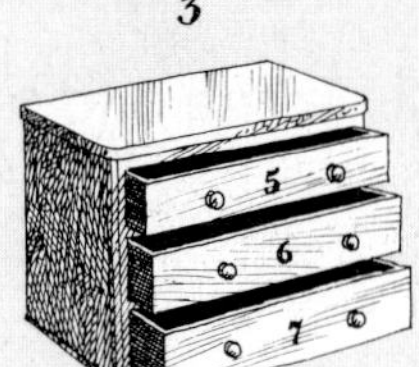

5

Put *in* or *on* in the sentences.

1 The glue is .... the top shelf .... the right.
2 Your socks are .... the middle drawer.
3 St Tropez is .... the south of France.

Reading

1

Read the following questions and answer them by reading the text.

1 Is ballroom dancing popular in Britain, according to the text?
2 How old are the children in the competitions?
3 Does Dr Hange like the competitions for children?

Young or old?

Ballroom dancing and the ten year old

Would you like your twelve-year-old daughter to be a dance champion? Does your ten-year-old son want to dance every day and at weekends? Are competitions good for children? A report by Leslie Stark. Photograph by Laura Scott.

Ballroom dancing is incredibly popular in Britain and the adult champions are often local celebrities. But now the kids are dancing too. They start when they are five years old, learning the steps of the waltz and the tango, the quickstep and the paso doble. By the age of eight they are competing for medals, and the youngest entrants for the full competitions are only ten! The young girls wear expensive dresses covered in sequins and they are made up like forty-year-olds. The boys have elegant tail coats and serious faces. The music starts, the spotlights are on, and the child dancers are off to try and win the prizes.

Dr Emmett Hange, a child psychiatrist, is very worried by these child 'stars'. He thinks that children should be children. 'I do not agree with these competitions,' he says. 'Young children who look like 40-year-olds start to think like 40-year-olds!'

2

Answer the following questions.

1 Who wrote the magazine article?
2 Who took the photographs?
3 What four kinds of dance are mentioned?
4 What do the young boys and girls wear for these competitions?

Remember Directions and instructions

Can you tell me how to	get to the cinema? use this camera?

Take the	first second	turning on the	left. right.	It's on your	left. right.

First Then	look through the viewfinder press the button	and	focus the lens. wind on the film.

Smoking, eating too much + favourite food X

4 Bad habits

fry, grill, boil, bake

Heart disease kills more than a million people in the world every year. In Britain alone 170,000 die from the disease annually. There are three main reasons for this: smoking, a bad diet, and not taking enough exercise. Many people travel to work by car, bus or train and then sit down at work all day! The food they eat is unhealthy and they eat too much. In a typical British dish of sausages, chips and beans there is too much salt and too much sugar—an important ingredient in tinned food—and there are not enough vegetables. And there is not enough fibre in most meals. There are too many deaths from heart disease. We can reduce that number, but we have to change our habits.

1

Look and listen. Are these statements true or false?

1 Only 10,000 people in the world die annually from heart disease.
2 There is only one reason for heart disease.
3 Many people do not take enough exercise.
4 There isn't any sugar in tinned food.
5 Smoking can cause heart disease.

Language focus

2

Study the pictures.

3

Ask and answer, like this:

> Why does the woman have to stand in picture 1?
> —There are too many people.
> There aren't enough chairs.

4 Cue cards for sentences

Ask and answer about each other, like this:

What kind of food do you eat?
—I eat too much tinned food and not enough fresh vegetables.

1 She has to stand up.
people/chairs

2 She can't go skiing.
trees/snow

3 He can't go sailing.
speedboats/wind

4 He is going to be late.
cars/parking spaces

Go through food - distribute in pairs - pick up 2 cards
I eat too much / many - + not enough ...

Language focus

1

Look at the pictures.

1 suntanned
been to the south of France

2 happy
got married

3 crying
won a gold medal

4 in pain
broken her arm

5 worried
spent too much money

6 feeling terrible
eaten too much lunch

2

Ask and answer, like this:

> Why are the man and the woman happy in picture 2?
> —They've just got married.

Read and write

3

Read this postcard and answer the questions.

1 Who wrote the postcard?
2 Who is the postcard for?
3 Where is Rob at the moment?
4 Did Rob like the football match?
5 Why?/Why not?

4

Write a different postcard from Rob. Choose one of the things below that he didn't like.

1 a concert
too many people, too noisy
2 a lecture
not clear enough, too long
3 a programme on TV
too much violence, not enough humour
4 a swim
not warm enough, too crowded

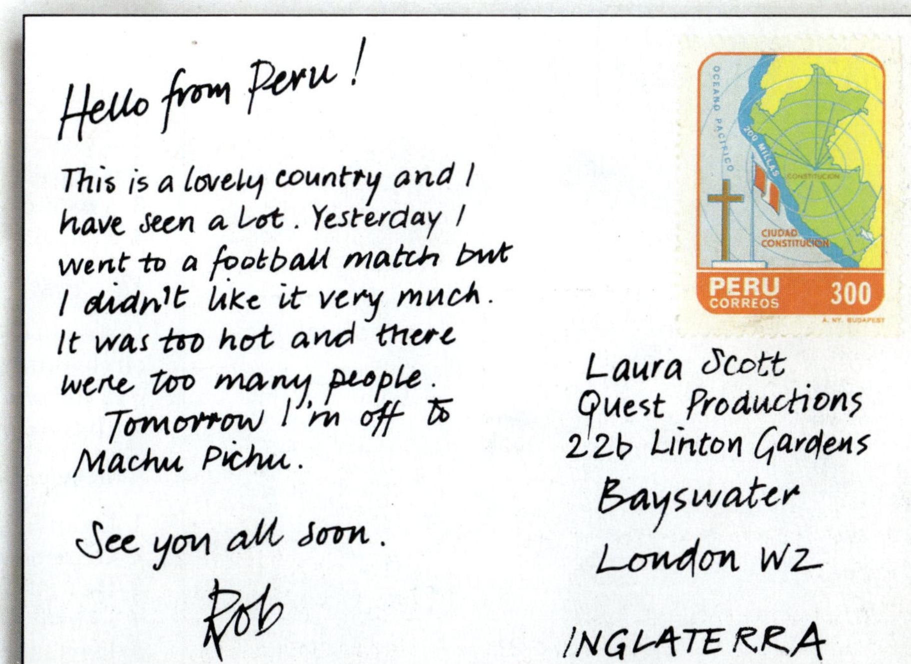

Hello from Peru!

This is a lovely country and I have seen a lot. Yesterday I went to a football match but I didn't like it very much. It was too hot and there were too many people.
Tomorrow I'm off to Machu Pichu.

See you all soon.

Rob

Laura Scott
Quest Productions
22b Linton Gardens
Bayswater
London W2

INGLATERRA

English in use: *Speaking*

1

Look and listen.

2

Have similar conversations, like this:

I'm	
Yes, it is rather ...., isn't it?	
Shall we ....?	
Yes, let's.	Not right now, thanks. (Maybe later.)

Here are some words to help you.

freezing	wet	have a drink
		put on some warm clothes
soaking	hot	open the windows
		have a swim
boiling	cold	go back to the house

Pronunciation

3

Listen to the cassette. Copy these phrases and underline the stressed syllables. Put two lines under the word with the main stress.

Example: a bottle of milk

1 a piece of cake
2 a cup of coffee
3 a pound of cheese
4 a carton of juice
5 a bar of chocolate
6 a box of matches
7 a packet of cigarettes

4

Listen to the cassette. Copy the words and put a circle round any words that have a sound like the *o* in the *pho* of *photographer*. Say the sentences with the correct stress.

Example: I'm going (to) buy (a) pound (of) cheese.

1 I want a cup of tea.
2 Give me a piece of cheese.
3 He's going to buy a pair of shoes.
4 I want to see a film.
5 I've just had a glass of milk.
6 I'm going to smoke a cigar.

Reading

1

Read the following questions and answer them by reading the text.

1 Who is Julia Collins?
2 What kind of person is her exercise plan for?
3 What different age groups is her exercise plan for?

2

Match the exercises with the pictures.

a running **b** touching your toes
c doing sit-ups **d** doing press-ups

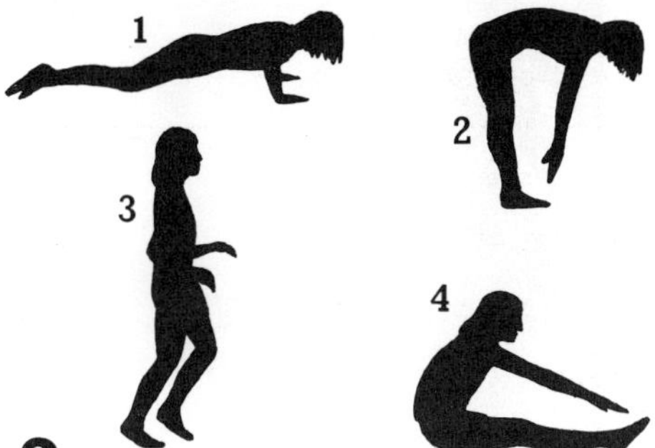

3

Complete the following exercise charts, based on Julia's plan.

	1st week	**2nd** week	**3rd** week
Age: 30–40			
running			
touching your toes			
sit-ups			
press-ups			

Age: 40–50			
running			
touching your toes			
sit-ups			
press-ups			

The Julia Collins Exercise Plan

Julia Collins is an Olympic downhill skiing champion. She trains for six hours every day and she is very fit indeed. We asked her to design a daily exercise plan for people who are not athletes. We also sent Adrian Hutton to take a photograph of Julia as she trained.

Here is my daily exercise plan. It's very easy. Look for your age group and start the programme.

If you are under 30:
For the first week run for ten minutes, touch your toes ten times and do ten sit-ups. During the second week run for ten minutes, touch your toes fifteen times, do ten sit-ups and ten press-ups. In the third week increase your running to twenty minutes and do five more of all the exercises.

If you are between 30 and 40:
Do the same running programme as the under thirties, but do five less of everything else.

If you are between 40 and 50:
Talk to your doctor before you start this programme
Do five minutes less running than the other groups. Run very carefully. Do ten less of everything else.

Next week: Julia's plan for weeks 4, 5 and 6.

Remember

There is	too much not enough	shadow. light.

There are	too many not enough	people. chairs.

NOTE: *enough* comes before a noun, but after an adjective, e.g.

I didn't have enough money. It wasn't warm enough.

The present perfect with 'just'

He/She	has	just	got married. been to the south of France. won the gold medal.
I/You/We/They	have		

5 Green hair

ALAN: Have you always been interested in photography?
CARLA: Oh, yes! I was given a camera for my eighth birthday.
ALAN: So you became a photographer immediately after school, I imagine?
CARLA: Oh, no. I did lots of different things.
ALAN: What kind of things?
CARLA: Well, I went to college and studied design. Oh, and once I was given a job at a hairdresser's.
ALAN: How long did you do that for?
CARLA: Not long. I was sacked after three weeks.
ALAN: Sacked? Why?
CARLA: I dyed a lady's hair green.
ALAN: What was wrong with that?
CARLA: She only wanted a haircut.

1

Look and listen. Answer the questions.

1 How did Carla get her first camera?
2 What did Carla study at college?
3 How long did Carla work at a hairdresser's?
4 Why did Carla lose her job at the hairdresser's?

Language focus

2

Look at the pictures and information opposite.
Alex Grunberg, the exiled scientist, talks about his life.

3

Ask and answer, like this:

What happened to Alex in 1983?
—He was awarded the National Science Prize.

4

Ask and answer about each other, like this:

Were you given any prizes at school?
—No, but I was made captain of the volleyball team.

They made me a professor in 1975.

They gave me a medal in 1980.

They made me head of the National Science Academy in 1982.

They awarded me the National Science Prize in 1983.

They dismissed me from my job in 1984.

They exiled me from my country last year.

Knocked down

1 My sister hit me.

2 That bicycle knocked me down.

3 My horse kicked me.

4 The police arrested them.

Language focus

1

Look at the pictures.

2

Ask and answer, like this:

> What's the matter with the old man in picture 2?
> —He's just been knocked down by a bicycle.

Read and write

3

Read the following and answer the questions.

These two people have just been rescued by the crew of a lifeboat. Their sailing boat was turned over by a large wave, but they got into their life raft and sent a distress signal. The lifeboat arrived half an hour later.

1 Who rescued the two people?
2 What turned over their sailing boat?
3 What did they do?
4 When did the lifeboat arrive?

4

Look at the pictures and write a similar paragraph about the girl.

rescued—*the mountain rescue team*

injured—*her rope broke*

her friends—*went for help*

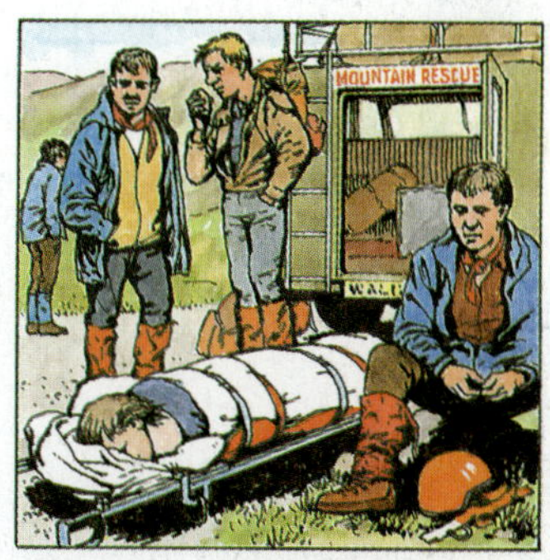

the mountain rescue team—*two hours later*

John Lennon, composer and writer of 'Imagine'.

Imagine all the people,
living life in peace.
You may say I'm a dreamer,
but I'm not the only one.

These words are from *Imagine*, one of the great songs of the 1970s. It was written and recorded by John Lennon. He was one of the Beatles. He was born in 1940 and he was killed by a madman in 1980.

Requiem

First performance: New York, 1985
Composer: Andrew Lloyd Webber (1948–) British.

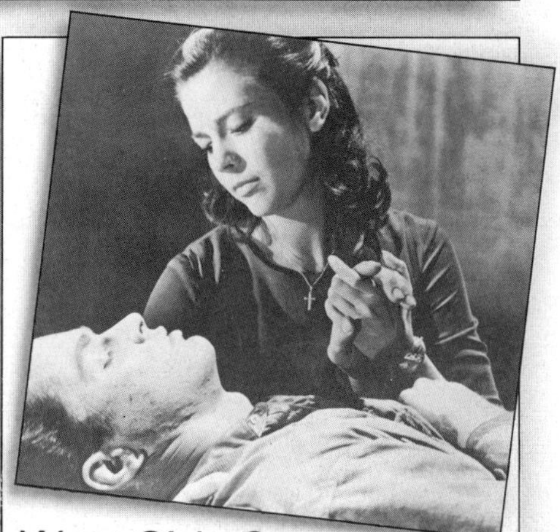

West Side Story

A modern version of the Romeo and Juliet story, set in New York.
Composer: Leonard Bernstein (1918–) American.

English in use:
Writing

1
Answer the following questions.

1 Who wrote *Imagine*?
2 When was John Lennon born?
3 How did John Lennon die?

2
Look at the information opposite.

3
Write sentences about *Requiem* and *West Side Story* starting with *He* and *It*.

1 *Requiem* was first performed in New York in 1985.
It ....
He ....

2 *West Side Story* is a modern version of the Romeo and Juliet story, set in New York.
It ....
He ....

4
Now write similar paragraphs about music, books, inventions, etc.
Example:

One hundred years of solitude is one of the great Latin American novels of this century. It was written by Gabriel Garcia Marquez. He is Colombian, but he lived for many years in Mexico.

Vocabulary work

5
Write the following numbers as figures.

Example: Two hundred and fifty.
250.........

1 One million.
2 Three hundred and two.
3 Two and a half million.
4 Eight thousand, two hundred and twenty.
5 One and a quarter million.

6
Say the following numbers.

1 250
2 903
3 5,300
4 1,500,000
5 1.75 million
6 2,700
7 1,250,000
8 3,410

1

Read the following questions and answer them by reading the text.

1 What is Dinorwig?
2 Where is Dinorwig?
3 Which natural resource does Dinorwig use?

DINORWIG

Underground power

Making the tunnels

If you fly over the Snowdonia National Park in Wales you can look down on two small lakes, Llyn Peris and Marchlyn Mawr. From your aeroplane you will see the peaceful lakes and the beautiful countryside around them. On the surface nothing has changed in this corner of Britain.

But underneath the hills is the most fantastic power station in the United Kingdom. It can supply 1,300 megawatts of electricity in just ten seconds. During the day, water from the top lake, Marchlyn Mawr, flows under the hills (and through the Dinorwig system) and ends up in the bottom lake, Llyn Peris. As the water flows through the hills electricity is generated by the giant turbines beneath the ground. At night, when there is less demand for electricity, water is pumped back up to Marchlyn Mawr.

The building of Dinorwig was the biggest engineering project in Britain for a long time. More than three million tonnes of rock were removed and sixteen kilometres of tunnels were dug inside the hills. The main machine hall at Dinorwig is probably the biggest man-made cavern in Europe. Dinorwig can supply one and a half million people with electricity for more than five hours. But from the air you would not even know it was there.

2

Which of the diagrams, **a** or **b**, refers to the daytime?

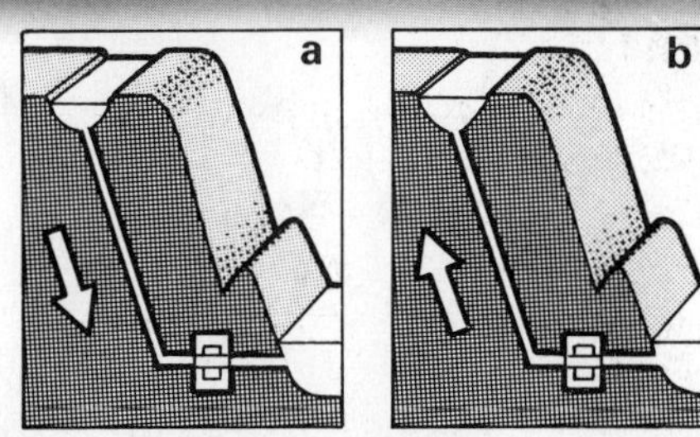

3

Answer the following questions.

1 How many megawatts are produced by Dinorwig in ten seconds?
2 How many tonnes of rock were removed?
3 How many kilometres of tunnels are there under the hills?
4 How much electricity can Dinorwig supply?

Remember The passive

You/We/They	were have (just) been	injured rescued met	(by	a wave). the police). Alan Sheerness).
I/He/She/It	was has (just) been			

Laura's story (1)

Cover text - look at picture

Laura usually leaves the offices of *Quest Productions* at about five o'clock, but last Monday she left at half past five. She wanted to get home by 6.30 and she ran to the bus stop but she couldn't get on a bus. There were too many people and not enough buses. Laura was desperate to get home so she decided to go by tube.

In the station she went to one of the automatic ticket machines but she didn't have enough change, so she had to join the queue at the ticket window. She bought her ticket and ran to the escalator. Laura went to the platform and waited for the tube. It arrived and the crowd moved forward.

Laura was pushed into the train. It was almost full but she was offered a seat by a man with a moustache. She thanked him but gave the seat to an old lady instead. Laura started to read her newspaper. In the tunnel the train stopped suddenly and she was thrown to the floor. Somebody screamed. The lights went out. It was quarter past six on a cold, wet December evening.

1

Look and listen. Ask questions about Laura's story using *how*, *what*, *what time*, *who*.

Language focus

2

Ask and answer, like this:

> Why did Laura go home by tube?
> —Because there weren't enough buses.

(Ask about *by bus*, *the automatic ticket machine*.)

3

Ask and answer, like this:

> What happened to Laura on the platform?
> —She was pushed into the train.

(Ask about *in the train*, *in the tunnel*.)

4

Have you ever arrived home very late because of a breakdown or an accident? Tell your story. - in 2 groups x3 - report to class

Jim's letter

1

Read these two letters and answer the questions that follow.

1. Who wrote the letter from
   a Linton Gardens?
   b Culver Drive?
2. Why is Jim going to go to *Quest Productions*?
3. When does Carla want Jim to go to *Quest Productions*?
4. When does Jim want to go to *Quest Productions*?

Quest

22B Linton Gardens, Bayswater, London W2

15th October

Dear Mr Daley,

Thank you very much for your letter of 28th September. Could you please come for an interview on Tuesday 22nd October at 10.30 a.m.?

I look forward to hearing from you.

Yours sincerely,

Carla Leone

Carla Leone

26 Culver Drive,
Islington
London N1
18th October

Dear Ms Leone,

Thank you for your letter of 15th October. I am afraid I cannot come for an interview on Tuesday 22nd October. Would Thursday 31st October be possible?

I look forward to hearing from you.

Yours sincerely,

Jim Daley

Language focus

2

Answer the following questions.

1. Carla wants Jim to go for an interview. What words does she use?
2. Jim doesn't want to go to *Quest Productions* on 22nd October. What words does he use?
3. Carla and Jim expect letters from each other. What words do they use?

Note: If Jim wanted to go on 22nd October he would write:
I will be happy to attend the interview on 22nd October at 10.30. I look forward to seeing you then.

3

Pairs A writes to B

Write a letter to a friend or colleague. Invite them to one of the following:

a meeting
a conference
an interview
an audition

4

B replies to A + vice versa.

Reply to the letter.

Jim's interview

Carla Leone is interviewing Jim Daley at *Quest Productions*. Jim is applying for the job of darkroom technician.

CARLA: Please sit down. Would you like a cup of coffee?
JIM: Yes, please.
CARLA: How do you take it?
JIM: White with two sugars, please.
CARLA: Adrian, could you get Mr Daley's coffee?
ADRIAN: Sure.
CARLA: Why do you want to work with *Quest Productions*?
JIM: Well, I've always wanted to work in a cooperative. I'd like a job with independence and responsibility.
CARLA: Have you ever worked in a darkroom before?
JIM: Oh, yes. I worked with the *Superphoto* company for two years.
CARLA: Why did you leave?
JIM: I was made redundant.
CARLA: I see.

1

Look and listen. Answer *yes* or *no*.

1 Does Jim want a job at *Quest Productions*?
2 Is Adrian going to get some coffee for Jim?
3 Has Jim worked in a darkroom before?
4 Did he leave his job because he was sacked?

Language focus

2

Look at the following interview questions.

Have you ever worked as a .../in ... before?
Why do you want to work in .../ as a ...?
Why did you leave your last job?

3

Look at the chart opposite. What questions can you ask to get the information?

4

Have interviews for one of the following jobs. Copy and complete the chart.

secretary
shop manager
cameraman
journalist
tour guide
air stewardess

NAME: ....
AGE: ....
ADDRESS: ....
....
MARITAL STATUS: ....
....
ABILITIES: ....
....
PREVIOUS EXPERIENCE: ....
....
....
REASONS FOR WANTING THE JOB: ....
....
....

Laura's story (2)

1

In this newspaper article the printers have left out some words by mistake. Which of the following words go into the blanks?

lights
repaired
turn on
photographs
terrible
reached
passengers
power

Power cut!

At 6.15 last night all the tube trains on the Bakerloo and Northern lines of the London Underground system suddenly stopped. A few seconds later, all the .... went out. Hundreds of people were trapped in the darkness.

One passenger said, 'It was ....! We sat there for more than an hour. It got hotter and hotter, and we got more and more frightened.'

The problem was caused by an electrical failure at a South London .... station which supplies power to the Northern and Bakerloo lines.

On one train the .... were led to safety by the train's guard. He told them to walk between the rails and he guided them to Regent's Park station. Afterwards he said, 'It was very frightening. I kept thinking, "Are they going to .... the power again?" Imagine 300 passengers walking between electric rails!'

The passengers all .... the safety of the station. One of them was photographer Laura Scott and she took some photographs of their 'walk'. 'Luckily I had my flash with me,' she said. 'So I took a few .... The guard was really fantastic. He deserves a medal!' The power system was .... after three hours and the trains started moving again half an hour later.

2

Answer the following questions.

1 Why did the trains stop?
2 Who helped the passengers on Laura's train?
3 At what time did the trains start moving again?

3

Look at this map of London's Underground system. Which line was Laura's train on, the Northern or the Bakerloo?

Bakerloo Line	Jubilee Line
Central Line	Metropolitan Line
Circle Line	East London Line
District Line	Northern Line
Piccadilly Line	British Rail
Victoria Line	

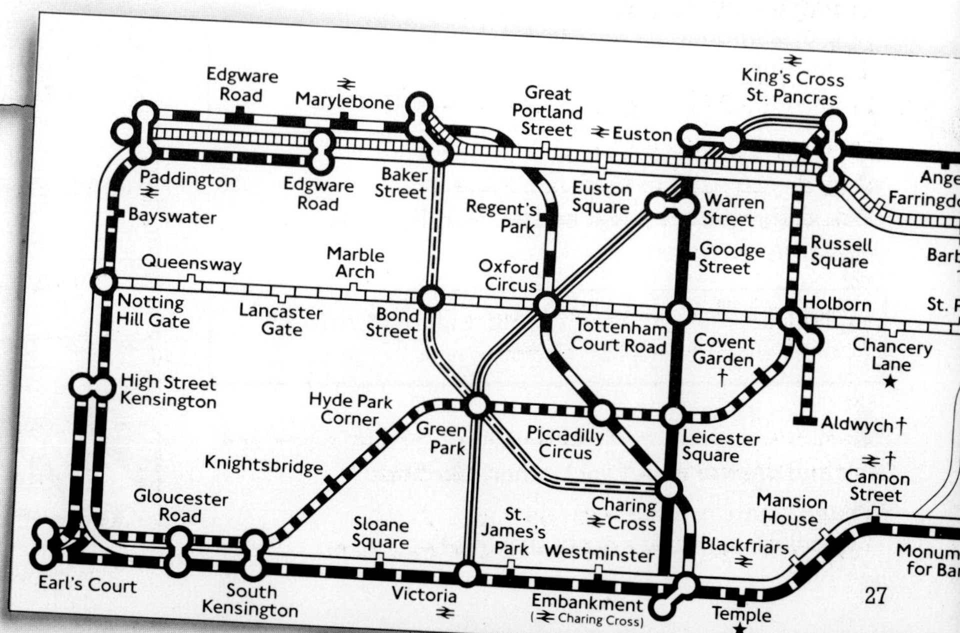

7 Machu Pichu

LAURA: Hello, Rob! Welcome back! Did you enjoy your trip?
ROB: Yes, I did. I saw some fantastic sights in Peru.
LAURA: Did you see Machu Pichu?
ROB: Yes, I did. It's incredible! It's high up in the mountains and you can still see the ruins of temples and houses from four hundred years ago.
LAURA: How do you get there?
ROB: On a little train. It looks very old, and it's rather slow. But it gets you there!
LAURA: What did you like best about the trip?
ROB: Oh, Machu Pichu, definitely.
LAURA: What about the food?
ROB: It didn't look very nice, but it tasted delicious!

1

Look and listen. Answer *yes* or *no*.

1 Has Rob just returned from Peru?
2 Is Machu Pichu a modern city?
3 Did Rob like Machu Pichu?
4 Is the train fast?
5 Does Rob like Peruvian food?

Language focus

2

In column **B** find the opposite of the adjectives in column **A**.

A	B
cheap	happy
sad	expensive
rich	fast
old-fashioned	poor
comfortable	modern
slow	uncomfortable

3

Look at the pictures. Ask and answer, like this, using *very*, *quite* or *rather*:

What can you say about the old man in picture 5?
—He looks rather poor, and very sad.

4

Ask and answer about each other, like this:

What's your car like?
—It looks fast, but it's quite slow really.

Language focus

1

Look.

It tastes
It smells
It looks

2

Ask and answer about the pictures, like this:

> What do you think of snails?
> —They look horrible (, but they taste delicious).

Read and write

3

Read the two paragraphs and answer the questions.

> Yesterday I bought a new sofa. It looks expensive but actually it was quite cheap. I like it and it is very comfortable.

> On Tuesday I met a man called John. He looks quite young, but actually he's quite old. He's very intelligent and good-looking.

1 Is the sofa expensive or cheap?
2 Is the sofa comfortable or uncomfortable?
3 Describe the sofa.

4 Is John young or old?
5 Is John good-looking or ugly?
6 Describe John.

4

Write a similar paragraph about someone you met, or something you bought, like this:

(Yesterday) I .... It looks ....
but actually .... I like ....
(and/but) ....

7 Welcome home

Rob Greenall returned from Peru last weekend. He found these three notes at his flat.

> Hello Rob!
>
> I hope Peru was fun. Please give me a call as soon as possible. If not... see you on Monday.
>
> Laura.

> Quest To: Rob Greenall
> From: Carla Leone
>
> Welcome back from Peru! I hope you had a good time. Please show me your photos as soon as possible.
> See you on Monday.
> Carla.

> FROM THE DARKROOM...
> Welcome home, Rob! Please bring your negatives from Peru first thing on Monday morning.
> See you then!
> Jim

English in use: *Writing*

1

Answer the questions.

1 Who wants Rob's photographs?
2 What does Laura want?
3 When does Carla want to see Rob's photos?
4 When does Jim want Rob's negatives?

2

Look at these two sentences.

I hope Peru was fun.
I hope you had a good time.

Now make similar sentences from these questions.

Example: Did you have a good time?
I hope you had a good time.

1 Were you happy?
2 Did you arrive on time?
3 Was your holiday fun?
4 Are you comfortable?
5 Did you catch your train?

3

Look at these sentences.

Please give me a call as soon as possible.
Please bring me your negatives first thing on Monday.

Write similar sentences. You can use these expressions.

write	me	a note
send	John	a letter/report
give		a call/ring

4

A friend or colleague arrives home after a journey. Write him or her a note like the note to Rob.

Vocabulary

5

GET can be used like an auxiliary in passive constructions. Read the passage and put one of the following in each space.

divorced knocked down engaged
married delayed

6

Write sentences about yourself or people you know using the following verbs with GET.

divorced engaged married
delayed knocked down

Sir Monty Starr talks about marriage. 'Many people get 1.......... too young. They don't have the experience that is necessary for marriage. I think young people should get 2.......... and then wait for a year or two – then they can decide. I will never get 3.......... "Once married, always married," I say.

But I nearly missed my wedding. I got 4.......... in heavy traffic on the way to the church. And then I got 5.......... by a boy on rollerskates just after the wedding. I was in hospital for the first two days of my married life! But that was twenty-five years ago, and they've been twenty-five wonderful years!'

Reading

1

Read the following questions and answer them by reading the text.

1 What is Cusichaca?
2 Who ruled Peru 500 years ago?
3 Why did the Inca civilization die?
4 What has happened in Cusichaca recently?

Water for Cusichaca

Ann Kendall

High up in the Andes mountains of Peru the past has been re-created. Indian families are again working in the fields of their Inca ancestors. Caroline Knight tells the story. Photographs by Rob Greenall.

Cusichaca: a lesson from the past

Cusichaca is the name of a village high up in the Andes mountains of Peru. Five hundred years ago there were nearly two thousand people living there. Now there are only fifteen families.

Five hundred years ago the Incas ruled Peru and their civilization was very advanced. They built cities like the beautiful Machu Pichu and the Inca capital, Cuzco. They had a complex system of roads all over the country. And at Cusichaca they grew food for the cities nearby.

When the Spanish invaded Peru, the Inca civilization died and Cusichaca died too. The land became dry and infertile and the Indians left the area. Now all that is changing. An archaeological team, led by Ann Kendall, has re-opened the old Inca canals which brought water down to the fields from the tops of the mountains. Indian families are working in the fields again, and the traditional crops of maize and beans are being grown. The past has solved the problems of the present.

2

Answer the following questions.

1 How many people live in Cusichaca now?
2 Who is the leader of the archaeological team?
3 Where does the water come from for the fields?
4 What are some of the traditional Inca crops?

Remember

Describing things

It	looks tastes smells	horrible. fantastic.
They	look taste smell	

It looks	very quite rather	expensive.

Hope

I hope	you had a good time. you are going to visit us. you are feeling well.

8 Juno and Neptune

ROB: Good morning. I'm Rob Greenall from *Quest Productions*.
WOMAN: Ah, yes. You want to take some photographs of our dolphins, don't you?
ROB: Yes, please.
WOMAN: Well, here they are. Meet Juno and Neptune.
ROB: They're incredible. Which is which?
WOMAN: The one nearest you is Neptune, and the one behind him is Juno. She's smaller than Neptune.
ROB: How intelligent are they?
WOMAN: Well, Juno seems to be more intelligent than Neptune, but they are both good at their tricks.
ROB: How much did they cost?
WOMAN: A lot! Juno cost me £250,000.
ROB: And Neptune?
WOMAN: Oh, he was cheaper. He was only £180,000.
ROB: And are they happy here, do you think?
WOMAN: I'm not sure. But they give a lot of pleasure to a lot of people.

1

Look and listen. Are these statements true or false?

1. Juno and Neptune are dolphins.
2. Neptune is bigger than Juno.
3. Neptune seems to be more intelligent than Juno.
4. Neptune was more expensive than Juno.

Language focus

2

Study the information about the two parrots.

3

Ask and answer like this, using the words in the box.

> Which is older, Ludwig or Frederick?
> —Frederick.

old	young	expensive
big	small	intelligent
cheap		

4

Ask and answer about other things, like this:

Which is more expensive, a Ford or a Rolls Royce?
—A Rolls Royce.

Language focus

1

Look at the information about these two hotels.

Palace Hotel		Sea View Hotel
□■■■■	comfortable	■■□□□
□□■■■	modern	■□□□□
□□□□■	quiet	■■■□□
□□□■■	clean	■□□□□
□□□□■	small	■■■■□
□□□□■	cheap	■■■■■
□□□■■	friendly	■■■□□

2

Use the words in the box to make statements like this:

> The Palace Hotel is more comfortable than the Sea View Hotel.
> The Palace Hotel isn't as quiet as the Sea View Hotel.

big	expensive
small	comfortable
quiet	uncomfortable
noisy	modern
cheap	old-fashioned

Read and write

3

Read Michael Horridge's article about Mediterranean hotels.

1 In what ways is the Palace Hotel 'better' than the Sea View Hotel?
2 In what ways is it 'worse'?

4

Complete Michael Horridge's article.

Mediterranean Hotels

by Michael Horridge. in the small Mediterranean town of Santa Teresa.

There are two hotels on this part of the coast, the Palace Hotel and the Sea View Hotel. They are very different, and so I am going to describe them both.

The Palace Hotel is certainly more modern than the Sea View Hotel and the rooms are more comfortable. Life at the Palace Hotel is noisier than at the Sea View but there are more amusement facilities. A room at the Palace Hotel is not as cheap as a room at the Sea View, but many people prefer it. The Sea View Hotel, on the other hand,

8 Giving advice

English in use: *Speaking*

1

Look and listen.

2

Look at this way of asking for and giving advice and offering reasons for that advice.

Shall I .... or ....?
—If I were you I'd ..../I wouldn't ....
Why?
—Because it's more ..../it isn't as .... as ....

3

Have conversations like Rob and Adrian about one of the subjects below.

Advantages of travel . . .	
by train:	comfortable/safe/reliable/cheap
by bus:	comfortable/interesting/convenient
by plane:	safe/quick

Advantages of buying . . .	
the 'Zoom' racket:	cheap/light
the 'Power' racket:	strong/heavy

Advantages of buying a house . . .	
in the country:	quiet/peaceful
in the town:	interesting/convenient

Pronunciation

4

Listen to the cassette. Put a line under the stressed syllables in the sentences. Repeat the sentences.

1 It looks lovely, but it tastes horrible.
2 It looks cheap, but it's very expensive.
3 They look happy.
4 It's old-fashioned, and it's very uncomfortable.
5 It smells delicious, but it tastes horrible.

5

Look at these sentences. Underline the syllables you want to stress. Now say the sentences.

1 They look horrible, but they taste delicious.
2 She looks sad, but she's very happy really.
3 It looks expensive, and it is.
4 It smells awful, but it's delicious.
5 They look rich, but I don't think they are.

Reading

1

Answer the following questions by reading the text.

1 How are dolphins caught?
2 What did Mark Petty think of the dolphin hunt?
3 What is life like for dolphins and killer whales in captivity?

The most popular attraction

Since 1970 at least sixty dolphins and twelve killer whales have been imported into Britain. Of these only eighteen dolphins and six killer whales have survived. Why is this? Karen Miller reports. Pictures by Rob Greenall.

Dolphins and killer whales are some of the most intelligent creatures on this planet. They are also the most popular attractions in many zoos and there are special 'Dolphinariums' all over the world in places like Tokyo, Miami, Mexico City and Sydney. The dolphins, together with killer whales and seals, perform for delighted crowds. They jump into the air, play football, wear enormous glasses and even 'sing' for the public.

Many of the dolphins that go to zoos and dolphinariums are hunted in the Gulf of Mexico and the Caribbean. They are chased by boats and planes and caught in nets. Then they are not given any food until they are prepared to eat dead fish, the food they are going to eat in captivity.

Mark Petty, an animal expert, went on a hunt for dolphins and was shocked. 'It was the worst thing I have ever seen, and certainly the cruellest,' he says. 'The dolphins were frightened and exhausted. Three of them died in the nets and two more were badly injured.'

Life for dolphins and killer whales in captivity is not much fun, either. They are kept in small tanks and they suffer from heart failure and infectious diseases. Some are even killed by visitors. At one zoo, in England, a dolphin called Sinbad died when a child threw a coin into his blow-hole.

2

Find the following information from the text.

1 How many dolphins and whales have died in Britain since 1970?
2 What 'animals' do the public like best in zoos?
3 How many dolphins died on the hunt, according to Mark Petty?
4 What three reasons are given for the death of dolphins and whales in captivity?

Remember Comparatives

Which is	bigger, older, more intelligent, more expensive,	Juno	or	Neptune?

<table>
<tr><td rowspan="2">The Palace Hotel
The Sea View Hotel</td><td>is</td><td>more expensive
more comfortable
cleaner
cheaper</td><td>than</td><td rowspan="2">The Sea View Hotel.
The Palace Hotel.</td></tr>
<tr><td>is not as</td><td>old-fashioned
modern
uncomfortable
noisy</td><td>as</td></tr>
</table>

9 Rob's car

CARLA: This is the slowest car I've ever been in! I can cycle faster than this!

ADRIAN: It's the noisiest car I've ever travelled in!

ROB: Come on! It's not that bad—especially in this weather.

LAURA: Well I like it. It's got the most comfortable seats I've ever sat in. Where did you get it, Rob?

ROB: My brother bought it in Germany. It was the cheapest car he could find.

ADRIAN: But why is it such a wreck? German cars are usually much better than this.

ROB: Not when they've had sixteen previous owners!

1

Answer the following questions with *yes* or *no*.

1 Is Rob's car fast according to Carla?
2 Does Adrian think that the car is very noisy?
3 Does Laura think that the seats are very comfortable?
4 Is Rob owner number seventeen?

Language focus

2

Look at this information about some of the members of Samson's Circus.

3

Ask and answer, like this. Use the adjectives below.

> Who's the strongest person at Samson's Circus?
> —Mike Russell.

strong tall ugly old young beautiful handsome

4

Ask and answer about other people, like this:

Who's the most intelligent member of your family?
—My brother.

The noisiest party

Language focus

1

Look at the pictures and repeat the words.

2

Ask and answer, like this:

> Why is the man going to call the police in picture 2?
> —Because it's the noisiest party his neighbours have ever had.

3

Ask and answer about each other, like this:

What's the most interesting book you've ever read?
—Empire of the Sun.

Read and write

4

Read the following, then copy and complete the chart about the *Blue Moon* shipping line.

The *Blue Moon* line has four ships, the *Star*, the *Comet*, the *Orbit*, and the *Eclipse*. The oldest ship is the *Comet*, and it is also the most comfortable. The most modern ship of the line is the *Eclipse*, and it is the fastest too. According to passengers, the *Orbit* goes on the most interesting cruises and it has the best food. It is also the most expensive.

5

Now write a similar paragraph about the *Calm Water* line using the information in the chart.

Name of the line:	BLUE MOON	Calm Water
Names of ships:		Topic, Lion, Breeze
Oldest ship:		Topic
Most comfortable ship:		Lion
Most modern ship:		Lion
Fastest ship:		Breeze
Most interesting cruises:		Breeze
Most expensive ship:		Topic

SAPPHIRE TOURS

TRY SAPPHIRE TOURS: WE'VE GOT THE HOLIDAY FOR YOU.

* If you like beaches, fly to Acapulco. It's the most famous resort in Mexico.
* If you like adventure, take the Trans-Sahara expedition. It's the most exciting trip in our brochure.
* If you like mountains and fresh air, travel to Zermatt. It's the most beautiful town in Switzerland.
* If you like sightseeing, go to Paestum. It has the most interesting ruins in Italy.

English in use: *Writing*

1

Complete these publicity stickers by reading the advertisement.

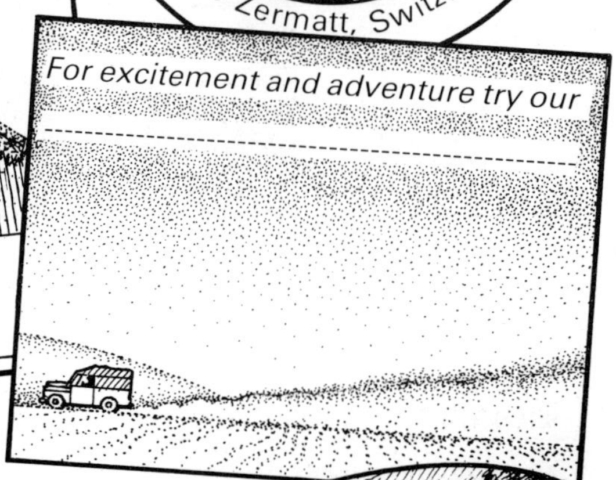

2

Answer these questions.

1 What is the most famous resort in your country?
2 What can you see at this resort?
3 How can you get to this resort?

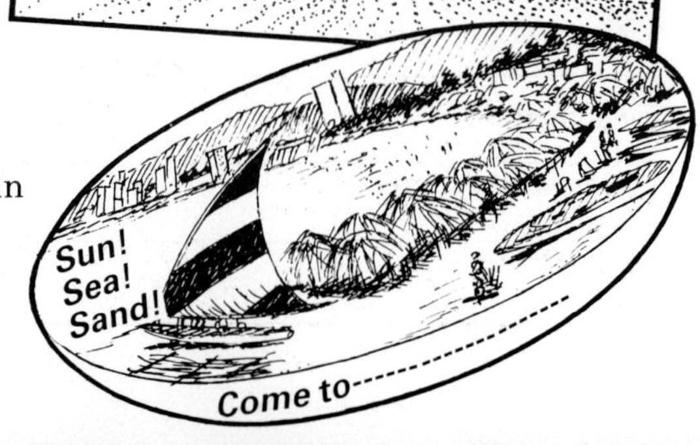

3

Write a sentence about a resort in your country, like this:

If you like ...., ... to ...., the most famous resort in ....

4

Write an advertisement for your own travel agency like the one for Sapphire Tours. You can use this information.

Beaches:
Miami Beach, Florida
St Tropez, France

Sightseeing:
Venice, Italy
Cappadocia, Turkey
Delphi, Greece

Adventure:
Himalayan expedition
Antarctic expedition

Beauty/peace:
The Lake District, England
Kashmir, India

Vocabulary work

5

Use a dictionary to check the meaning of these words. Then give them the opposite meaning by adding un- or in-.

Example: kind—*unkind*

happy	interesting
intelligent	convenient
expensive	safe
exciting	comfortable
reliable	pleasant

6

Make the superlative forms for each pair of adjectives.

Examples: kind—*kindest*
unkind—*most unkind*

7

Make sentences with the adjectives, like this:

.... is the (most) ....
.... I've ever ....

Reading

1

Answer these questions by reading the text.

1 What is Terry Connell's job?
2 Does Terry like his job?
3 What is the best thing about being a model?
4 What would Terry like to do in the future?

PROFILE

Our reporter talks to Terry Connell, the well-known model. Photographs by Laura Scott.

TERRY CONNELL ***model***

Q: How long have you been a model?
A: For about two years now.
Q: What sort of work do you do?
A: Well, I'll do just about anything. I've just done some swimwear advertisements and tomorrow I'm starting a week's work at a hairdressing salon.
Q: Do you like modelling?
A: Oh, yes. It's always exciting and interesting, and the best thing about it is that you travel all over the place. And it's better than being a bus conductor! But there are problems, too.
Q: What are they?

A: The worst thing is that you are always putting on and taking off clothes, shoes, hats, gloves, scarves, glasses—anything that can be worn. And of course you have to look after your body—you can't eat and drink what you want and you must keep fit. But it's the best job I've ever had, so I'm not complaining.
Q: How did you become a model, Terry?
A: I was working as a London bus conductor at the time. One day a photographer was taking some cosmetics photographs on the buses. He asked me to stand with the model in one shot and I agreed. I didn't think anything of it. Two weeks later I got a phone call from the same photographer. Would I like to become a model? I said yes! That was two years ago.
Q: One last question, Terry. What are you going to do when you stop modelling?
A: I don't really know. Maybe I'll go and live on an island. If I have enough money, I'll buy one!

2

Answer the following questions.

1 What do models have to do?
2 What was Terry's previous job?
3 What was Terry's first modelling experience?
4 How long has Terry been a model?

Remember Superlatives

worst best	biggest oldest ugliest noisiest	most	beautiful intelligent expensive (un)reliable

It's the	most interesting biggest worst	book elephant concert	I've ever	read. seen. been to.

Rob's story (1)

Here is the news, read by Julie Jones.

Police and rescue teams from three countries are searching the Sahara Desert for a party of tourists on a Trans-Sahara expedition. They were last seen by some wandering tribesmen a week ago, but they have not contacted anyone since then. The Algerian authorities believe that the tribesmen saw the expedition about 500 kilometres south of Figuig.
The expedition has five landrovers, six drivers and fifteen travellers, among them Rob Greenall, a photographer from *Quest Productions*.

1

Look and listen. Ask and answer questions about the text using *who*, *when*, *how many*, and *where*.

Language focus

2

What is your favourite kind of holiday? Why?

3

Study the information about these three tours.

4

Compare the three holidays, like this:

> Is the English Canals holiday as expensive as the Trans-Sahara expedition?
> —No, it isn't.
> Which is the most comfortable holiday, do you think?
> —The Atlantic Cruise, I imagine.

5

Ask and answer about each other, like this:

Which of the three holidays would you like to go on?
—I think I'd prefer an English Canals holiday.
Why?
—Well, I don't like the idea of crossing the Sahara, and the canal holiday is the cheapest of the three.

Figuig

1

Read this postcard which Rob sent to his colleagues at *Quest Productions*. Answer the questions that follow.

1. When did Rob arrive in Figuig?
2. Where is Figuig?
3. Where is the group staying?
4. When is Rob going back to *Quest Productions*?

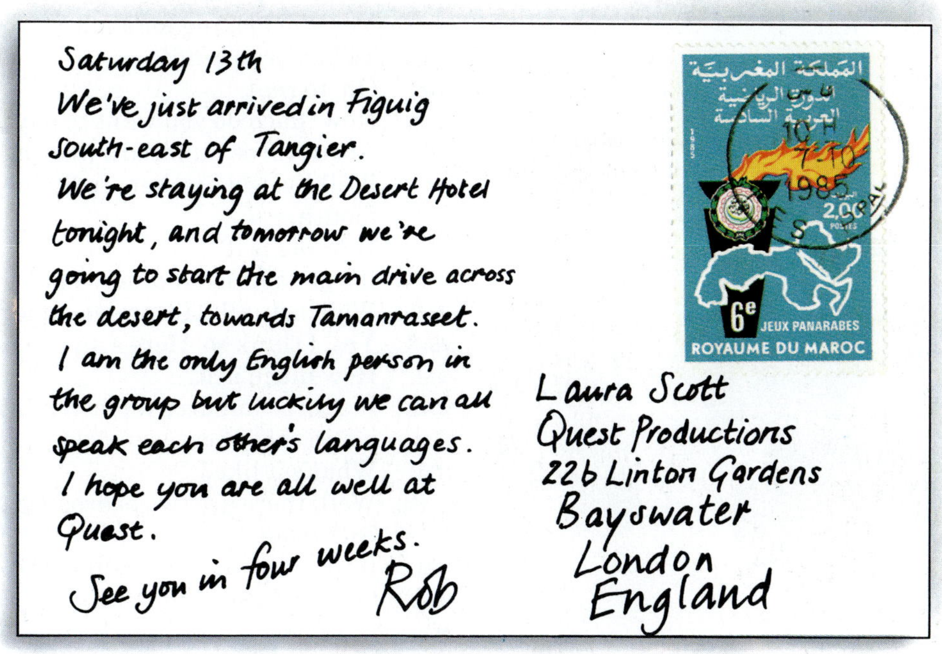

Saturday 13th
We've just arrived in Figuig south-east of Tangier.
We're staying at the Desert Hotel tonight, and tomorrow we're going to start the main drive across the desert, towards Tamanrasset.
I am the only English person in the group but luckily we can all speak each other's languages.
I hope you are all well at Quest.
See you in four weeks.
Rob

Laura Scott
Quest Productions
22b Linton Gardens
Bayswater
London
England

Language focus

2

Three search parties have set out to look for the Trans-Sahara expedition:
a Moroccan team (orange line),
an Algerian team (blue line)
and a Malian team (green line).

Ask and answer, like this:

> Where are the Moroccans?
> —They've just arrived at Bechar.
> Where is Bechar?
> —It's south-east of Fes.
> How far have they travelled?
> —About 350 kilometres.
> How far is it from Bechar to Adrar?
> —About 500 kilometres.

points of compass
it's north of etc.

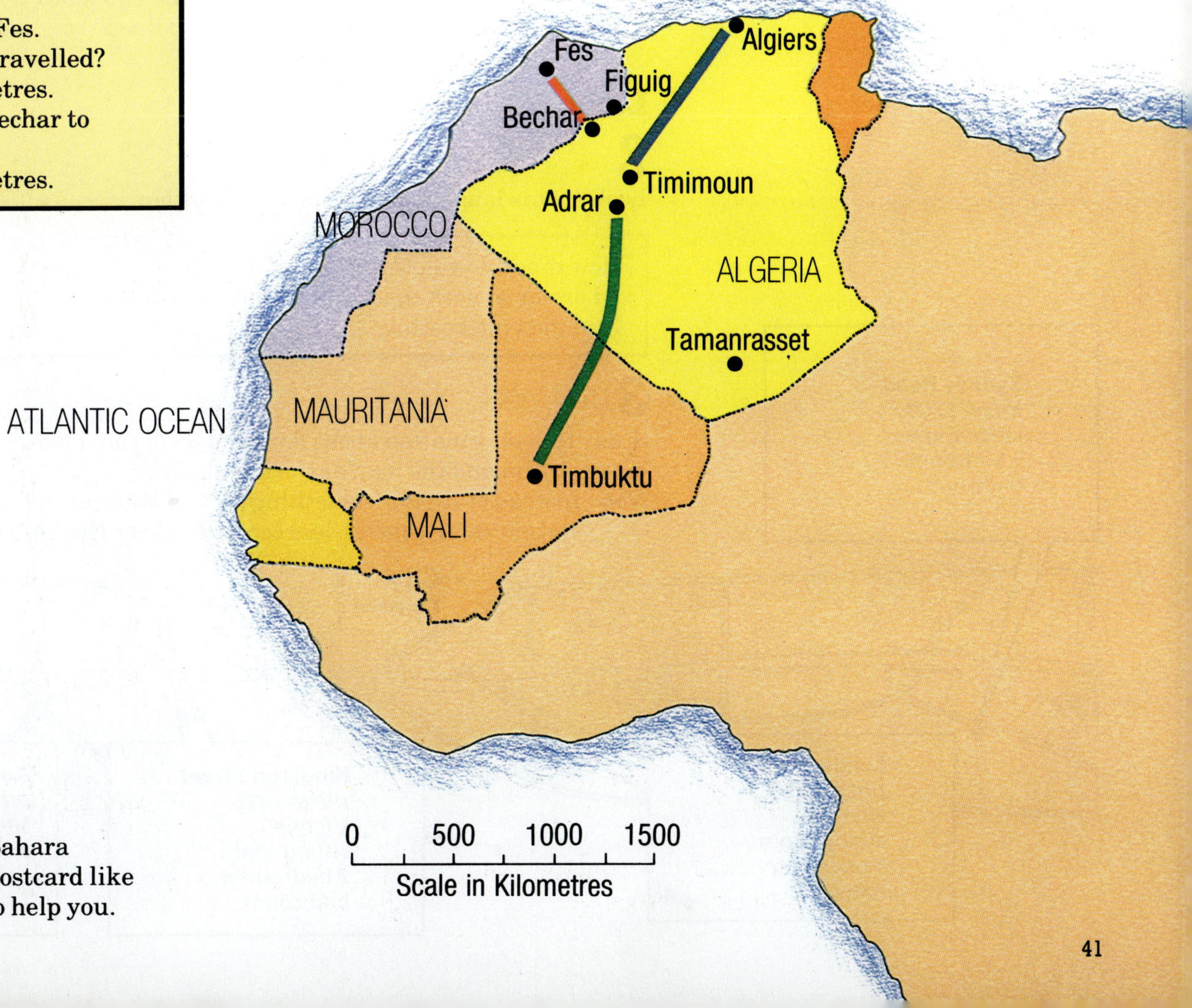

Writing

3

You are on a Trans-Sahara expedition. Write a postcard like Rob's. Use the map to help you.

Flat hunting

MAN: Can I help you?
JIM: Yes, I'm looking for a flat.
MAN: To buy or to rent?
JIM: Oh, to rent.
MAN: How much do you want to pay?
JIM: About three hundred a month.
MAN: Well I've got one here in Sydney Road. It's two hundred and sixty a month.
JIM: How big is it?
MAN: It's got a kitchen-diner, a bathroom and one bedroom.
JIM: Well, actually, I'd prefer something a bit bigger if that's possible.
MAN: Yes, I think so. Here's an interesting one. It's opposite the park.
JIM: How much is it?
MAN: It's three hundred and twenty-five a month. It's the biggest flat we've got in this area.
JIM: What's it like?
MAN: Well, there are two bedrooms, a sitting room, a kitchen and a bathroom.
JIM: It sounds very interesting. Can I go and see it?
MAN: Of course, sir. Can I have your name and address?

1

Look and listen. Answer the questions.

1 Which is the cheapest of these three?
a the price Jim wants to pay **b** the price of the flat opposite the park
c the price of the flat in Sydney Road
2 How many rooms are there in each of the two flats? S. Road 3 Park 5
3 Why doesn't Jim like the flat in Sydney Road? too small

Task Listening - looking for a flat

Language focus

2

Look at this language from the conversation.

> How much do you want to pay?/How big is it?/How much is it?
> I'd prefer something bigger if that's possible.
> It sounds interesting.

3

Study this information about flats and have conversations like the one between Jim and the man at the flat agency.

Note: Instead of saying 'something bigger' you can say 'something nearer the station/more central/less central/nearer the centre', etc.

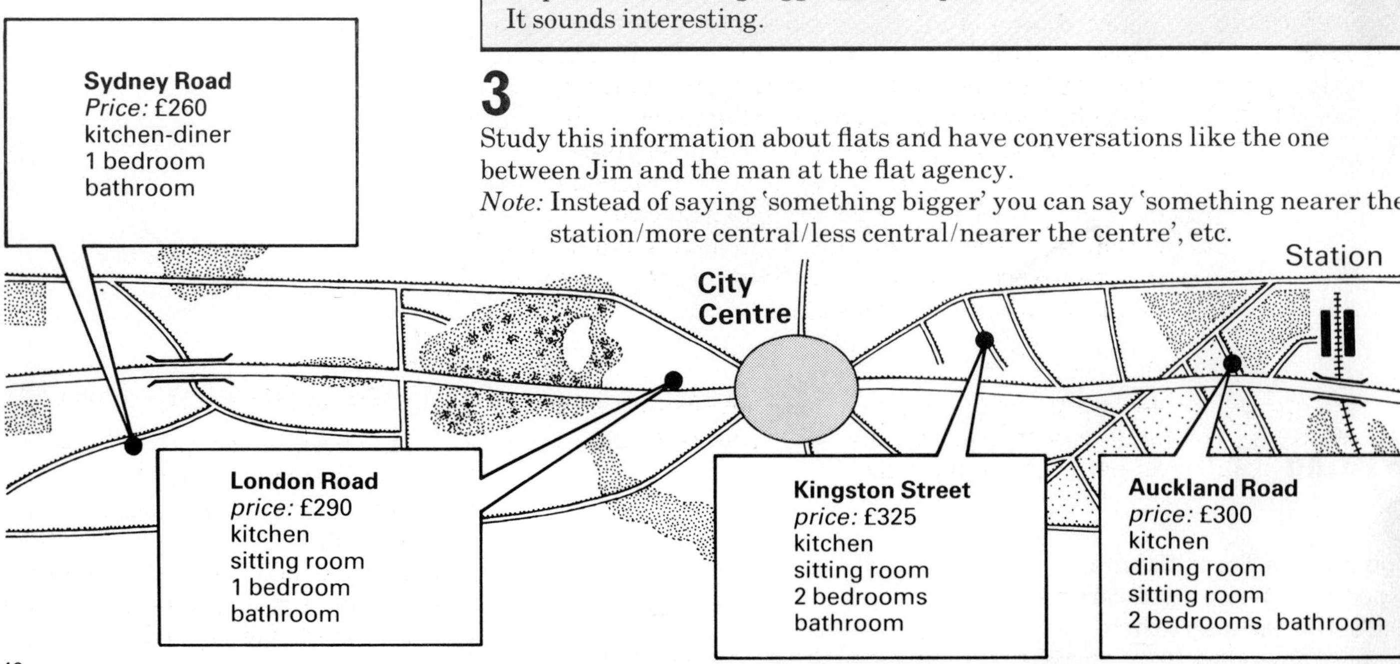

Rob's story (2)

1

Rob's diary of his experiences on the Trans-Sahara expedition is going to be printed. The printers have got some of the diary mixed up. The dates are in the right places, and so are paragraphs **A** and **D**. But the other paragraphs are mixed up. What is the correct order?

Monday 16th (A)

Today we saw some nomadic tribesmen. They were all on camels. We tried to talk to them, but they got away as fast as they could. But I think I've got some good photos of them.

Wednesday 18th (B)

We are safe! At about eight o'clock this morning a helicopter from the Algerian army flew overhead and the pilot saw us. About an hour later we were rescued. Now I am going to have my first hot bath for three weeks. I can't wait!

Thursday 19th (C)

The two front landrovers crashed into each other this morning and both were damaged quite badly. Ali, the expedition leader, decided to abandon them and so we all got into the remaining three vehicles.

Sunday 22nd (D)

We've been here since Thursday trying to repair the landrovers. I don't know what we're going to do. Our radios don't work and we are running out of water. The only good thing for me is that my cameras were not damaged in the storm. But we must be rescued soon . . .

Wednesday 25th (E)

We were driving along in the remaining three vehicles at about 10 this morning when one of them broke down. Ali worked for three hours but he couldn't repair it. We were talking about what to do when a sandstorm struck us. There was sand everywhere—we couldn't see anything and we soon had sand in our eyes, our nostrils, our equipment and our supplies. The storm lasted for three hours and when it was over we found that none of the landrovers would work. We are really in a mess!

Thursday 26th (F)

What is going to happen to us? I haven't had a drink for twelve hours. If we are not found soon, somebody's going to die.

2

Answer the following questions.

1 How many landrovers did the expedition start with?
2 Who was the leader of the expedition?
3 How long did the sandstorm last?
4 At what time were the members of the expedition rescued?

11 Island paradise

Laura Scott has flown to a desert island to take photographs of Keith Rogers. Keith is alone on the island as an experiment.

LAURA: Hello. You're Keith, aren't you?
KEITH: Yes, I am. Who are you?
LAURA: I'm Laura Scott. I'm a photographer.
KEITH: From England?
LAURA: Yes. How long have you been here, Keith?
KEITH: Since 30th January. But what's the date today? You see my watch has stopped.
LAURA: 29th June.
KEITH: 29th June! That means I've been here for six months!
LAURA: Is there anything you miss, Keith?
KEITH: Oh, yes! I haven't spoken to anyone for six months and I haven't had a cup of tea since the end of February.
LAURA: But you like the island, don't you?
KEITH: No, I don't! I hate it! I've hated this place ever since I arrived. Take me back to civilization!

1

Look and listen. Are these statements true or false?

1 Keith has been alone on the island since 30th January.
2 It is now 29th June. Keith has not had a cup of tea for six months.
3 Keith has enjoyed his six months on the island.
4 Keith wants to leave the island.

Language focus

2

Read the following and give the correct dates for the pictures.

Stella and Sam Samson are the owners of Samson's Circus. They also own a castle in Scotland on the shores of Loch Lomond. They moved to Scotland three years ago and they bought the castle last January. Stella and Sam first met each other twenty-six years ago. They got married two years later.

3

Ask and answer, like this:

How long have they owned the castle? —Since January./For (three) months.

4

Ask and answer about each other, like this:

How long have you been a student?
—For eleven months./Since January.

Language focus

1

Read the following paragraph and study the information.

In India there is a custom of sannyasin. Some men, when they are old, leave their families and their homes. They give up all their possessions and become religious men, called sannyasins. They wander all over the country and beg for food. Anrit Bangar became a sannyasin. He left his house six years ago.

1 He last spoke to his family six years ago.

2 He last wore shoes five years ago.

3 He last ate fish seven years ago.

4 He last watched television six years ago.

5 He last listened to the radio five years ago.

6 He last travelled by train three years ago.

2

Ask and answer, like this:

> Does Anrit ever wear shoes?
> —No, he hasn't worn shoes for five years.

Read and write

3

Read the paragraph opposite. Are the statements about it true or false?

1 Sam Samson is the manager and owner of Samson's Circus.
2 Sam became the manager sixteen years ago.
3 The circus went on a tour of Russia last month.
4 The Samsons like their castle.

The owners of Lomond Castle

The owners of Lomond Castle are Stella and Sam Samson, of Samson's Circus. Sam Samson has been the manager of Samson's Circus for twenty years and the owner since 1981, although his brother still has shares in the company. The circus has been very successful and is off next month for a tour of Russia. The Samsons say they like Lomond Castle very much and expect to stay there for a long time.

4

Use the following notes to write a similar report about the Bangar family.

COME BACK SAYS SANNYASIN'S WIFE

Mrs Shalini Bangar - wife of Anrit, a sannyasin - wants him back.
Anrit - a sannyasin - 6 years - his family - not talked to him since then - saw him - Delhi station - three years ago.
Family - unhappy - going to look for Anrit again.

11 The theatre

Last week Laura was feeling bored. She wanted to go out, so she bought the local paper and looked at the 'What's on' page. She didn't want to go to the cinema because people are allowed to smoke there and she doesn't like the smell. She didn't want to go to a rock concert, either, so she looked at the theatre section. There she saw an advertisement for a play by Alan Ayckbourn. She's always liked Ayckbourn's plays, so she booked a seat for the performance that evening.

ARTS THEATRE
Box Office 352000 · Credit Cards 316421
Nightly at 8 (Sat Mat 4.30) Oxford Playhouse Company
in Alan Ayckbourn's latest comedy success
WAY UPSTREAM
"Hilarious knockabout comedy" — Financial Times
28th Jan-2 Feb, Marius Goring and Paul Darrow in
J. B. Priestley's
I HAVE BEEN HERE BEFORE

★ Rock concert with **THE BUZZ** at the Triangle Club
7.30 tonight. TICKETS AT THE ENTRANCE ★

ARTS CINEMA Tel: 352001
Thurs 24th only at 2.00 & 11.00 pm, Nastassja Kinski and Malcolm McDowell in Paul Schrader's **CAT PEOPLE (18)**
Thurs and Friday at 4.00, 6.15 & 8.30, Vanessa Redgrave, Christopher Reeve and Madelaine Potter in James Ivory's **THE BOSTONIANS (PG)** from the novel by Henry James
Fri at 2.00 & 11.00 pm (Sat at 11.30 pm) The Talking Heads in **STOP MAKING SENSE (PG)** Presented in Dolby Stereo and with a new powerful amplification system!

ABC CAMBRIDGE 64537

1 Today, Friday 25th & Saturday 26th Steven Spielberg presents **GREMLINS (15)** Zach Galligan, Phoebe Cates Sep Perfs: Week 2.00, 5.00 & 8.00 Sunday, 27th January for 5 days Tim Thomerson, Helen Hunt **TRANCERS (15)** Progs: 1.50, 3.25 & 6.55. Sun 3.25 & 6.55	**2** Today & Friday 25th January for 7 days Peter Shaffers presents **AMADEUS (PG)** Separate performances Sun 7.15 only. Week 2.00 & 7.15

VICTORIA CAMBRIDGE 352677

1 Today & Friday 25th January, for 7 days **GHOSTBUSTERS (PG)** 1.30, 4.35, 7.35. Sun 4.30, 7.35 Prog comm: 2.00, 5.00, 8.05. Sun 5.00, 8.05	**2** **REVENGE OF THE NERDS (18)** Prog comm 2.45, 6.45 From Sun 27th for 5 days only **GREMLINS (15)** Week 2.00, 5.00, 8.00. Sun 5.00, 8.00

Vic 1: Late Show, Friday 25th January **CHRISTINE (18)**
Late show Saturday 26th January **REVENGE OF THE NERDS (18)**
Vic 2: Late Show, Friday 25th January **PICK-UP GIRLS.**

English in use: *Writing*

1

Look at the text and the advertisements above and answer the questions.

1 Why did Laura buy the local paper?
2 Why didn't Laura want to go to the cinema?
3 Why did she look at the theatre section?
4 Why did she book a seat?
5 What was the name of the play?
6 What time did it start?

2

Join the following pairs of sentences with *because* or *so*.

1 I arrived late for the play. I missed the first ten minutes.
2 I didn't want to spend a lot of money. I didn't buy the special programme.
3 The man in the next seat got angry. I tripped over him on the way to my seat.
4 I liked the main actress. She was very funny.
5 I was very tired. I fell asleep.
6 The man in the next seat shouted at me. I was snoring.

3

Write about a story like Laura's about a television programme you saw recently. Use the following expressions:

I wanted to ....
I didn't want to ....
I've always/never liked ....
(and) so ....
because ....

Vocabulary work

4

Write one of the following in the sentences.

into up out of to off on

1 She got _____ the car.

2 They got _____ the bus.

3 He got _____ the taxi.

4 He gets _____ at 6 o'clock.

5 She got _____ the bus.

6 He gets _____ work at 9.15.

5

Write sentences about you, using the following verbs:

get up get out of get on
get into get off get to

Reading

1

Answer the following questions by reading the text.

1 How did Lucy meet Gerald?
2 Where did they go together?
3 Why did they get ill?
4 Why did they get better?
5 What did Lucy do at the end of the year?

Castaway!

Lucy Irvine was twenty-five when she saw an advertisement in a newspaper. 'Writer seeks wife for a year on a tropical island.' She answered the advertisement and met Gerald Kingsland, the writer. Soon they were married and they went to look for their island paradise. They found it in the Torres Strait, between Australia and New Guinea. It was called Tuin.

Lucy and Gerald were the only people on Tuin, and for a long time they saw nobody. They caught fish and drank water from a fresh-water spring. They planted vegetables: tomatoes, green beans and sweetcorn.

But life on the island was not easy. On the very first night Gerald was bitten by sandflies and his legs were soon infected. For a long time he could hardly walk.

Soon they had another worry. The rains were late, and the spring began to dry up. All their vegetable plants died. They drank only half a cup of water a day and ate only fish. They became very ill, thin and weak. Their island paradise had become a nightmare.

Lucy and Gerald were very lucky. They were visited by people from Badu Island. The islanders gave them food and medicine and they got well again.

When the year finished Lucy said goodbye to Tuin, and she also said goodbye to Gerald. She went back to Britain on her own and wrote a book about her experiences on Tuin. She called it *Castaway*.

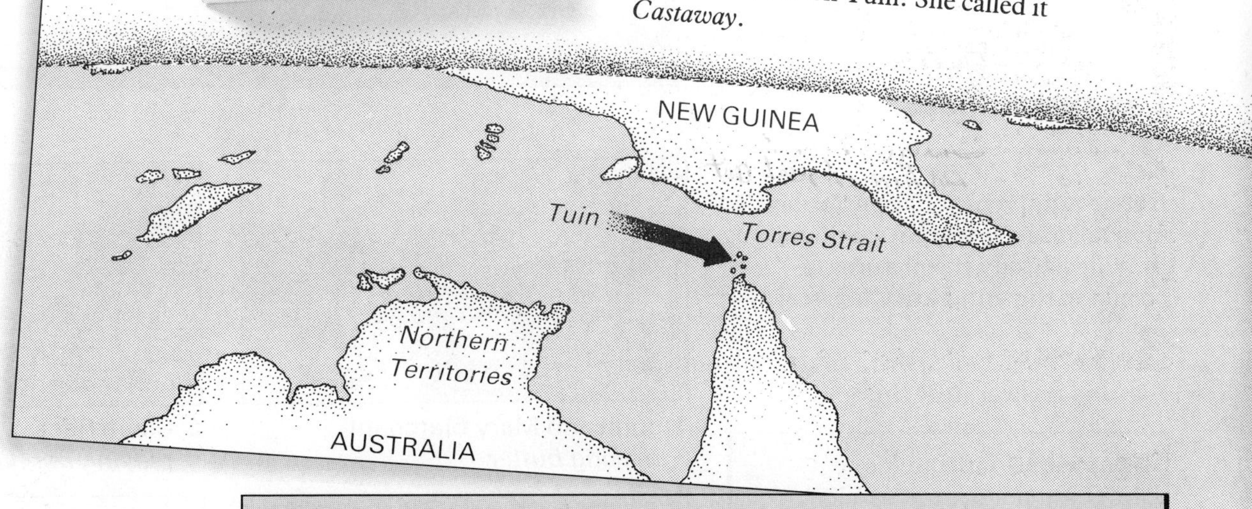

2

Answer the following questions.

1 Where is Tuin?
2 What vegetables did Lucy and Gerald plant?
3 What did they eat and drink when the plants died and the spring dried up?
4 Where did Lucy write her book?

Remember The present perfect with 'since' and 'for'

How long have you been a student?	Since	1986. last December.
	For	a year. six months.

She has not seen her grandmother	since	Tuesday.
	for	three days.

12 Bikini Atoll

James Cameron was one of the most famous journalists in Britain until his death in 1985. He wrote for many English newspapers and often appeared on television. He said, 'One experience changed my life. It was 9.00 a.m. on 24th July 1946. I was standing on an American ship with a lot of other journalists. We were in the South Pacific. We were all looking towards the horizon and waiting. We were wearing special black goggles. Suddenly there was a bright light—the brightest light I've ever seen. Later we heard the sound of an enormous explosion and saw a huge mushroom cloud. It was the most terrible thing I have ever seen.'

The place was Bikini Atoll. The journalists had witnessed America's first peacetime nuclear test.

1

Look and listen. Answer the following questions.

1 Who was James Cameron?
2 What were the journalists doing at 9 o'clock on 24th July, 1946?
3 What were they wearing?
4 What did they all see?
5 What did the explosion look like?

Language focus

2

Seen P. 77 picture of past cont.

At one minute past five yesterday afternoon there was an earthquake in Wales. Study the pictures of people in the village of Gladestry.

1 John and Mary Marchant
making butter

2 Claire Rees
playing her flute

3 Johnny and Sam Williams
fishing

4 Owen Thomas
feeding the hens

3

Ask and answer, like this:

> What were John and Mary Marchant doing at five o'clock yesterday afternoon?
> —They were making butter.

4

Ask and answer about each other:

What were you doing at eight o'clock last night?
—I was running. What about you?

Language focus

1

Last night at 9.30 the tent at Samson's Circus collapsed in the middle of a show.
Match the activities with the people in the picture.

swinging on the trapeze
riding an elephant
climbing a ladder
doing cartwheels
juggling

2

Ask and answer, like this:

> What was Elsa doing when the tent collapsed?
> —She was riding an elephant.

Read and write

3

Read the following and answer the questions.

> **Earth tremor shakes Welsh village**
> At one minute past five yesterday afternoon there was an earthquake in Wales. The tremor registered 3.2 on the Richter scale and lasted for ten seconds. The epicentre was the Welsh village of Gladestry. When the quake struck, Owen Thomas, a farmer, was feeding his hens. A mile away, John and Mary Marchant were making butter in their farmhouse when the floor began to shake.
> 'I was terrified,' said Mrs Marchant. 'The milk spilt and I thought it was the end of the world.'
> A number of plates were broken in Owen Thomas's farmhouse, but the police have not reported any injuries.

1 How long did the earthquake last?
2 Where was the centre of the earthquake?
3 Where were the Marchants when the earthquake struck?
4 What was broken in the earthquake?

4

Use these notes to write a similar report about the collapse of the tent at Samson's Circus.

```
TENT COLLAPSE AT SAMSON'S CIRCUS
A storm - the tent poles snapped
Mario Prelli - juggling - "I thought we were all
going to die. We were very lucky."
"The elephants were terrified" - Pauline Barnaby.
Tent completely destroyed. No serious injuries - police.
```

12 Plans

English in use: *Speaking*

1

Look and listen.

2

Look at these ways of talking about arrangements.

What are you doing ....?	
No plans Nothing special.	
Definite arrangements I'm	
Changeable plans I was planning to	
Would you like to ....?	
Accept (Yes.) That would be great.	*Refuse* I'd rather not, thanks.

3

Copy and complete the diary for next week. Write down two definite arrangements, two uncertain plans, and leave three days with no plans.

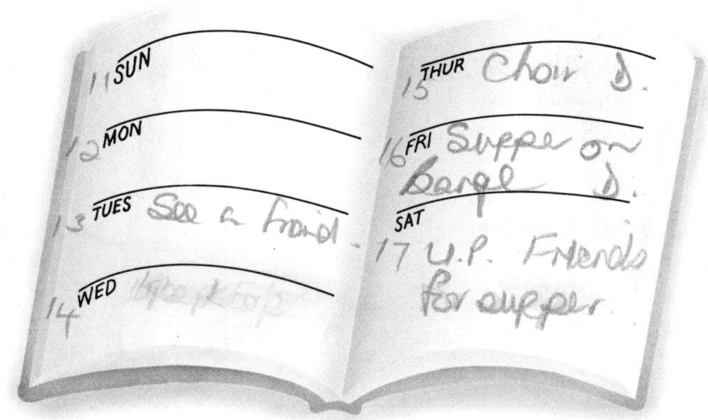

4

Use your diaries to have conversations like this:

What are you doing on Tuesday evening?
—I'm having a meal with a friend.
Oh. What are you doing on Wednesday?
—Nothing special.
Would you like to come to the cinema?
—Yes. That would be great.

Pronunciation

5

Listen to the cassette. You will hear some sentences. For each sentence say which word you hear, **a**, **b** (or **c**).

1	**a** ship	**b** zip	**c** sip
2	**a** shock	**b** sock	
3	**a** place	**b** plays	
4	**a** shoe	**b** zoo	**c** Sue
5	**a** buzz	**b** bus	
6	**a** shellfish	**b** selfish	

6

Say these phrases and sentences. Pay special attention to the pronunciation of *s*, *z*, and *sh*.

1 She sings well.
2 He likes music.
3 She won the first prize.
4 I haven't seen him since the summer.
5 She's shopping for shoes.

Reading

H.W

1

Read the following questions and answer them by reading the text.

1 What happens in and around El Paso?
2 What is special about the church?
3 Why can life be a bit frightening for inhabitants in the El Paso area?

The Church with a missile on top

Where can you find a school with a team called *The Rockets*? Where can you take your children to a Missile Park—full of old guided missiles? And where can you find a church which actually has a missile on top?

The answer is El Paso, an American city of 489,000 inhabitants. This is the centre of the American missile programme, and all kinds of missiles, both nuclear and non-nuclear are tested in the area. Missiles are everywhere in El Paso. People collect them and put them in their gardens. Their ashtrays are made from bits of old missiles, and farmers buy old missiles for their cows to drink water from!

If you live near El Paso, though, life can be a bit frightening! In 1947, for example, a rocket was fired and it flew north. Then, for some reason, it changed direction and flew back over El Paso. 'It made a noise like an express train,' said one old inhabitant of the city. The missile flew over the border and landed in the Mexican town of Juarez. Recently the Americans wanted to simulate a nuclear explosion. They used chemicals to make a mushroom cloud. It looked very realistic, but many people had not been warned about the simulated explosion. They saw the cloud and thought it was the start of World War III!

If you visit the area and feel nervous, please don't worry. You can always relax with a drink at the 'Missile Inn' hotel. The best drinks are in the 'Rocket Bar'.

2

Answer the following questions.

1 What three uses for old missiles are given in the text?
2 In which directions did the missile fly in 1947?
3 Where are the names 'Missile' and 'Rocket' used in the El Paso area?

Remember The past continuous

What	was	I/he/she/it	doing	when	the bomb went off?
	were	you/we/they			the telephone rang?

I/He/She/It	was	having a bath.
You/We/They	were	watching television.

13 A new bike

LAURA: Hey, is that new?
ROB: Yes. Do you like it?
LAURA: It's incredible. But how can you afford it?
ROB: Well, I had a bit of luck. Carla asked me to buy some special paper for her in North London. And after that I had a drink at a pub there.
LAURA: So?
ROB: Well, Greta Johnson was in there—
LAURA: You mean Greta Johnson, the actress?
ROB: Yes, that's right. She was with Ray Valence, the star of 'Troubled Times'. So I took some photos and then this man came up to me.
LAURA: What did he do?
ROB: He asked me to give him the film in my camera. I refused politely and asked him to explain.
LAURA: And did he?
ROB: No. He just told me to give him the film and gave me £200.
LAURA: Did you give it to him?
ROB: Of course!
LAURA: But the film was worth more!
ROB: I know! I sold the *other* roll to a magazine—for £1500!

1

Look and listen. Answer the following questions.

1 What did Carla say to Rob?
2 What did the man in the pub say to Rob first?
3 What was Rob's reply?
4 What did the man say then?

Language focus

2

Look at the pictures and say the words.

1 hijacker tell　　2 stewardess ask　　3 pilot tell　　4 steward ask

3

Ask and answer like this, using *ask* or *tell*.

> What did the stewardess ask the passengers to do?
> —She asked them to return to their seats.

4

Talk to each other, like this:

Juan, ask Maria to leave the room.
—Maria, could you leave the room, please?
What did Juan ask Maria to do?
—He asked her to leave the room.

Language focus

1

Read the paragraph and look at the pictures.

Fred and Wally were a famous comedy team. They made many films. In each film Fred told Wally what to do, but Wally couldn't do it.

strong/weak fat/thin rich/poor tall/short

2

Ask and answer, like this:

> What did Fred tell Wally to do in *The Journey*?
> —He told him to get the case.
> Why didn't he?
> —Because { he wasn't strong enough to carry it. / he was too weak to carry it.

Read and write

3

Read the following and complete the conversation.

The general asked the soldier to stop talking. The soldier told the general not to interrupt. The general told the soldier not to be rude.

GENERAL: ....
SOLDIER: ....
GENERAL: ....

4

Read this conversation and then write a similar paragraph about the fireman and the old lady.

Fireman: Could you leave your house, please?
Old Lady: Go away and leave me alone!
Fireman: Don't be silly!

13 Telex

```
1772938
625970
NO 1959/497
QUESTPRO LONDON

ATTN: LAURA SCOTT

POLITICAL SITUATION HERE WORSE STOP DECIDED TO STAY ON FOR WEEK
BUT RUNNING OUT OF MONEY STOP PLS TELL ADRIAN SEND MORE STOP

REGARDS
CARLA LEONE
625970 QUESTPRO
1772938 BRCOM
```

English in use: *Writing*

1

Answer the following questions.

1 Who is the telex to and from?
2 What is her problem?
3 What are her plans?
4 What does she want Adrian to do?

2

Telexes and telegrams are expensive and so people often miss out or shorten words. What words have been missed out or shortened in Carla's telex?

3

Look at the following sentence from the telex.

PLS TELL ADRIAN SEND MORE

In normal use she would say:
Please tell Adrian to send more.

Write Carla's sentences for the following situations both for normal use and for a telex.

1 She wants Adrian to fly there immediately.
2 She wants Laura to contact the Central Bank in Panama.
3 She wants Rob to meet her at Heathrow Airport.

4

Look at this sentence from Carla's telex.

(I have) decided to stay on for (a) week.

Here are some ways of conveying decisions.

I have decided to (do) ....
I am planning to (do) ....
I am thinking of (doing) ....

Now make sentences from the following:

1 stay on (possible)
2 fly to India (definite)
3 return in two days (probable)

5

You are Carla Leone. Send a telex to the *Quest Productions* office in London. Say what is happening, what your decision is, and what you want Adrian (or Laura or Rob) to do.

Vocabulary work

6

In each of the following groups of words find one word that does not fit and then say why.

Example: camera film lens drink viewfinder
drink—the other words are about photography

1 seat chair sofa ladder stool
2 castle aeroplane house flat bungalow
3 sugar honey salt pepper flour
4 comedy western horror documentary novel
5 priest stewardess pilot driver sailor

7

Now write your own groups of words and ask other students which word doesn't fit.

Reading

1

Read the questions and answer them by reading the text.

1 Who wrote the text?
2 Who did he write it for?
3 What are the three main points of the article?

CAMERA TIPS

Adrian Hutton's weekly column of advice for beginner photographers. This week—photographing people.

Here are my tips for taking good photographs of your family, friends and people who interest you.

Keep it simple—Don't have too much detail in your picture. Choose surroundings and backgrounds carefully—they should add to the picture, not take away interest from your main subject.

Shoot from higher and lower angles—Taking pictures of small children? Get down to their level. Kneel down so that your camera is at eye-level with the child (instead of aiming down). Taking photographs of a group of people? See if there are stairs nearby so you can shoot from a higher angle. Each person in the group will be more visible than if you shoot them at eye level.

Ask your subjects NOT to look at the camera—Pictures of people are usually much more natural-looking when they are doing something, and looking at what they're doing. When your subject has forgotten about the camera is when you'll probably get your best pictures.

These are my tips for good photos, but don't take my word for it! Try for yourself! And remember, don't be afraid to experiment.

Adrian Hutton

Get down to their level.

People are much more natural when they are doing something.

2

Answer the following questions.

1 What's the best way to take photographs of children?
2 When will you get your best pictures?
3 What must you not be afraid of?

Remember 'ask' and 'tell'

She The woman They	asked told	him the man them	to	clean the car. stop talking. sit down.

'too' and 'enough'

He is	too weak not strong enough	to	lift the suitcase. unscrew the bottletop.

14 Consolidation
Carla's story (1)

It was three o'clock in the afternoon. Carla was sitting in a cafe in Paestum, near the famous ruins, drinking a strong cup of coffee. She was writing a postcard to her colleagues at *Quest Productions*. A woman sat down at her table. Carla looked up. The woman wasn't Italian, but Carla did not know her nationality. The woman said, 'You're English, aren't you?' Carla said she was, and she and the woman started talking to each other. Then the woman asked Carla to help her. Carla agreed, and the woman asked her to take a present to a friend in England. She told her to wait at the Temple of Neptune that evening. A boy with a red scarf would meet her there.

Carla was puzzled. Who was the woman? Who was the boy? What was the 'present'?

That evening Carla went to the temple and waited for the boy with the red scarf. When he arrived, Carla was taking photographs in the evening sun. Carla turned round and said hello. Without a word, the boy took a small parcel out of a bag and gave it to Carla. They both started to walk away. At that moment two policemen stepped out from behind a pillar and told them to stop. Carla obeyed the order but the boy started to run away.

1
Look and listen. Ask and answer questions about the text using *who*, *what*, *when* and *where*.

2
Who is the most interesting person you've met on a holiday?

Language focus

3
Ask and answer about what Carla was doing, like this:

What was Carla doing when the woman sat down at her table?
—She was writing a postcard.
What did Carla do when the woman sat down at her table?
—She looked up.

4
Ask and answer, like this:

What was Carla told to do by the woman in the cafe?
—She was told to wait at the Temple of Neptune.

Ask about Carla and the woman, the boy and the policemen.

Werewolf!

It was night. There was a full moon. A boy and a girl were walking down the main street of a small town in Texas. The wind was whistling through the trees and the couple were walking as fast as possible towards the church at the end of the street. Suddenly a huge shape—half man, half wolf—rushed out of the shadows. The girl was killed instantly by a blow from the creature's enormous paw. The boy screamed and ran towards the church. He never reached his destination. The creature ran back into the shadows. The street was quiet again. Two clouds drifted across the moon.

'Cut,' shouted the director. 'We're going to do that again. John, you killed Mary too quickly!'

1

Answer the following questions.

1 Describe the scene before the incident.
2 Who or what killed the girl?
3 What happened to the boy?
4 Find two words in the text that mean 'big'.
5 Do you enjoy horror stories? Why?/Why not?

Language focus

2

Look at these stages for telling a story.

A State the time and the conditions.	*It was night. There was a full moon.*
B Give the background.	*A boy and a girl were walking . . .* *The wind was whistling . . .*
C Give the action.	*Suddenly a huge shape . . . rushed . . .* *The girl was killed instantly.*
D Conclude the incident.	*The street was quiet again. Two clouds drifted . . .*

3

Look at these pictures and tell their story in the same way.

4

Write your own story.
It starts with these words.

It was a black night . . .

The prize

PETER: Congratulations, Laura! You've won the London Photographic Prize for this year. How does it feel?
LAURA: Wonderful! I'm really happy.
PETER: Well, your pictures are very good. How long have you been a photographer?
LAURA: Not very long . . . for about three years.
PETER: And how many prizes have you won?
LAURA: Oh, this is the first, although I've entered quite a few competitions.
PETER: What's the most exciting photographic job you've ever worked on?
LAURA: Oh, definitely the Italian power boat race!
PETER: Yes, I saw those photos. They were excellent.
LAURA: Thank you.
PETER: What are your plans now, Laura?
LAURA: Well, next week I'm working with the Spanish National Ballet Company and after that I'm going to have a holiday.
PETER: You deserve one. Congratulations again, Laura!

1

Look and listen. Answer the questions.

1 What has Laura won?
2 Has Laura won any prizes before?
3 What is Laura doing next week?
4 What is she going to do after that?

Language focus

2

Look at this language from the conversation above.

How long have you been a photographer?
How many prizes have you won?
What's the most exciting assignment you've ever worked on?
What are your plans now?

3

Look at the following information.

NAME:	Jean Edwards	Gavin Samuels
OCCUPATION:	high jumper	ballroom dancer
ACHIEVEMENT:	British women's high jump record	First prize, World Championship
PREVIOUS WINS:	Gold medal, Commonwealth Games	Youth prize, British Championship
MOST EXCITING EXPERIENCE:	Winning the Commonwealth medal	Meeting the Queen
PLANS:	Get married Go to the Olympics	Go on holiday Go to university

Have conversations with Jean and Gavin like the one between Peter and Laura.

Carla's story (2)

1

In these two newspaper reports the printers have made some mistakes. Some lines are in the wrong place: when they should be in one report they are in the other! Find the lines.

English photographer in Italian drama

From our Italian correspondent

The Paestum authorities yesterday
thanked an English woman,
Carla Leone, for her help.
Carla, a photographer, helped the
police catch an international
gang of thieves. A woman asked
Carla to take a parcel to Britain.
Carla was suspicious and talked
to Oxford Circus tube station.
waiting when Carla met a male
member of the gang at a
ruined temple and the boy was
arrested. Later the other
monkeys escaped and jumped onto
as they were boarding a flight
to Lisbon. The parcel which the
boy gave to Carla contained two
monkeys were taken back to
the first century B.C.

Man takes monkeys in zoo drama

From our home affairs correspondent

In a bizarre incident yesterday
a man stole two monkeys from
Regent's Park Zoo. The man,
Darren Black, has a history of
mental illness and the police
think he took the monkeys to
attract attention. Black opened
the monkeys' cage and took them
to the Italian police. They were
Members of the public rang the
police. But Black took the
monkeys down the escalators and
onto the platform. One of the
members of the gang were caught
a train, but a woman with a banana
took it to the police. After a
chase Black was caught and the
Roman coins and a bracelet from
the zoo by their keeper, Alf
Chapman.

2

Are the following statements true or false?

1 Carla was arrested by the Italian police.
2 Darren Black stole two elephants from the zoo.
3 There were more than two members in the smugglers' gang.
4 Black took the monkeys to a bus station.
5 The boy at the temple gave Carla some very old Roman coins.
6 Alf Chapman wanted to attract attention.

15 The pass

GUARD: Hey! You mustn't go in there!
ROB: Why not?
GUARD: You've got a camera! It's against the rules.
ROB: Oh, I'm sorry. I didn't know that.
GUARD: Have you got a pass?
ROB: A what?
GUARD: A pass. You must have a pass if you want to go in there!
ROB: Well, I haven't got one.
GUARD: Then you'd better leave.
ROB: Wait. Where can I get a pass?
GUARD: In room 321.
ROB: Where's that?
GUARD: You go up those stairs and it's the third door on the left.
ROB: Thanks.
GUARD: Oi, where are you going?
ROB: To room 321.
GUARD: But you can't go there. You must have a pass if you want to enter the building, and you haven't got one, have you?

1

Look and listen. Answer *yes* or *no*.

1 Are cameras permitted in the building?
2 Is a pass necessary for this building?
3 Can you get a pass in room 321?
4 Is Rob going to get a pass, do you think?

Language focus

2

Study the signs opposite.

3

Ask and answer, like this:

> What does the sign mean in picture 4?
> —It means that you must not drive at more than thirty miles an hour.

4

Design a sign. Then ask and answer in the following way:

What does my sign mean?
—I don't know! I think it means that you must wait in the queue.

Great films

Language focus

1

Look at the pictures from some well-known films. Fill in the blanks with *must* or *don't have to*.

What did Sherlock Holmes say to Watson?
– He said, 'You don't have to come with me, but you must keep quiet.'

2

Ask and answer in the same way about conversations between the following people:

a head nurse to nurse;
b manager to shop assistant;
c cook to kitchen assistant.

The words in the box will help you.

Not necessary	Necessary
peel the potatoes wash the floors wear a uniform	wash the potatoes make the beds wear a tie

© 1986 The Walt Disney Company

Read and write

3

Read the notice and put O (obligatory) or NO (not obligatory) against these conditions.

1 Arrive before 9.00 a.m.
2 Report to the guards.
3 Sign in the book.
4 Wear badges.
5 Eat lunch in the building.
6 Tell guards of movements.
7 Be checked by guards.

INTERNATIONAL COMPUTERS:
NEW SECURITY ARRANGEMENTS
All employees must arrive before 9.00 a.m.every morning, and they must report immediately to the security guards. Employees must sign their names in the security book but they do not have to wear identification badges. They do not have to eat lunch in the building although they must tell the security guards of their movements. All employees must be checked by the security staff before they leave the building.

4

Use these notes to write a similar paragraph for employees of the Southern (nuclear) power station.

SOUTHERN NUCLEAR POWER STATION

OBLIGATORY
have radiation checks before they leave the power station
wear protective clothes at work
report to the security guards in the morning
no smoking in the power station

NOT OBLIGATORY
wear protective clothes in the canteen or the games room

POSSIBLE NEW HOUSES FOR THE NEW ENGLISH SCHOOL: A REPORT

There are two possibilities: Glebe House in Regent Street and number 37 Railway Road.

Glebe House is very attractive because it has four floors and it is an old Victorian building. But, although it is in a good part of town, it is not near any shops.

The house in Railway Road is a possibility because it is very near the station and it has a large garden. The rooms are very small, although the house itself is quite big.

CONCLUSION: Although the house on Railway Road is central and has enough rooms, I would recommend Glebe House because it is the right size and can accommodate a large school.

SIGNATURE: Peter G. Blake DATE: 2 January

a

b

English in use: *Writing*

1
Read the report.

2
Copy and complete this chart.

	ADVANTAGES	*DISADVANTAGES*
Glebe House		
37 Railway Road		

Which is the photograph of Glebe House?

3
Join the following pairs of sentences using *although* or *because*.

1 The house is not in good condition. It is in a nice area.
2 The school is very noisy. It is near the airport.
3 The hospital is not very comfortable. It is very old.
4 The food is delicious. The kitchen isn't very clean.

4
Look at the details of these two beaches. Write a report about which beach would be suitable for a new hotel. Use *although* and *because*.

	ADVANTAGES	DISADVANTAGES
Smuggler's Bay 	beautiful easy to get to	very rough sea small beach
Sunset Beach 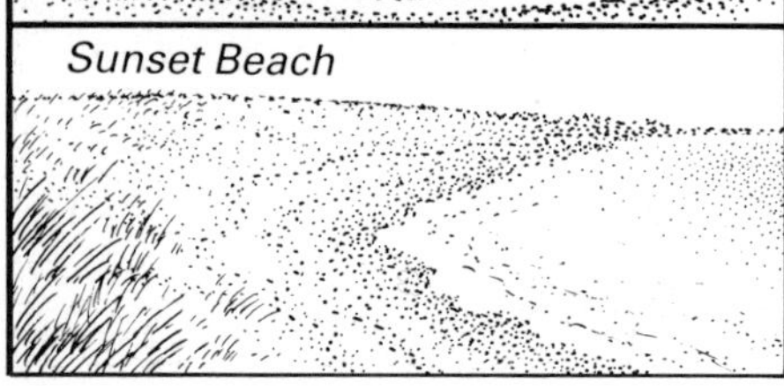	long sandy beach calm sea	rather flat no main road

Vocabulary work

5
Put the following words in three columns. Column A—for words that can only be used with *is*, column B—for words that can only be used with *are* and column C—for words that can be used with *is* and *are*.

people, the news, the team, the Royal Family, money, furniture, the police, the government, homework.

6
Choose the verb form in the following sentences. Both are possible in some cases.

1 The police is/are searching for the murderer.
2 Money is/are the thing most people want.
3 The government is/are studying the new information.
4 The news was/were very bad this morning.
5 English people doesn't/don't usually speak many languages.
6 Modern furniture is/are often uncomfortable.

Stop acid rain! 15

Reading

1

Read the following questions and answer them by reading the text.

1 What is acid rain?
2 What damage does acid rain cause?
3 Why is acid rain 'unnecessary'?

2

Answer the following questions.

1 When was the photograph on the right taken?
2 What future consequences of acid rain are mentioned in this poster?
3 According to the poster, how can we save our environment?

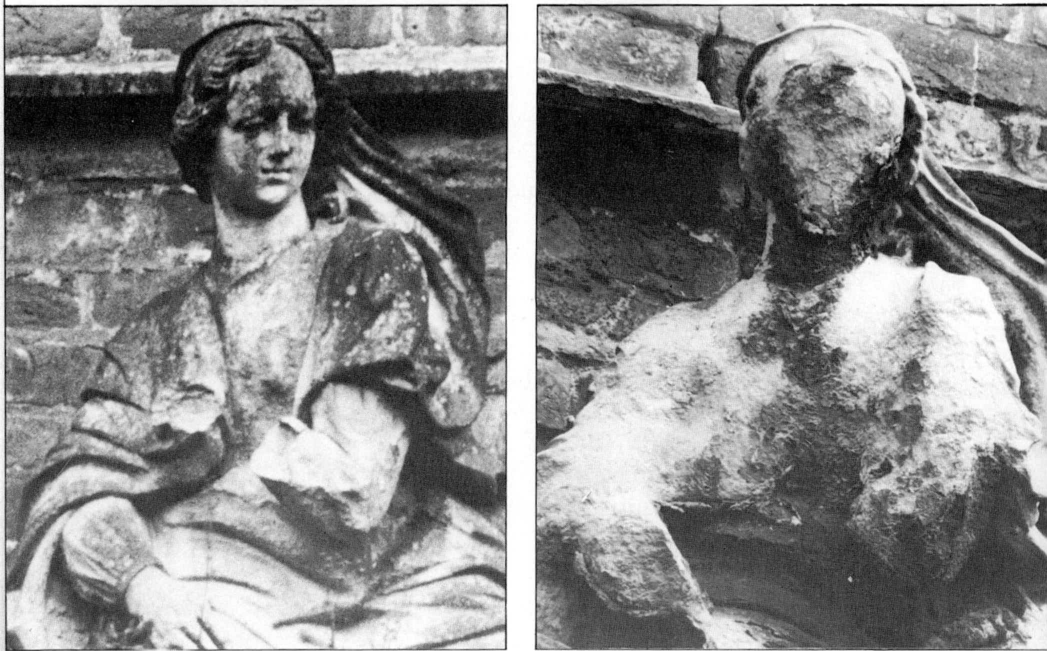

- The photograph on the left shows a stone figure from the walls of a castle in Germany. It was taken in 1908. The photograph on the right shows the same figure sixty years later. The damage has been caused by air pollution.
- Every year millions of tons of sulphur pour into the air from factory chimneys all over the world. In the air this sulphur is mixed with oxygen and becomes sulphuric acid. Then it falls with the rain. Acid rain.
- Acid rain poisons lakes and kills trees, and it eats into materials like stone. Already the fish have died in lakes all over Europe and the forests of Germany are full of dead trees.
- In the modern world acid rain is completely unnecessary! The smoke can be cleaned before it leaves the chimneys and cars can be better designed so they cause less pollution. But many governments don't want to do these things because they are too expensive.
- IF we go on producing acid rain the rivers and lakes of the world will die.

BUT . . .

- IF we control acid rain we can save our environment for our children and grandchildren.

Remember Obligation

<table>
<tr><td>I/You/We/They</td><td rowspan="2">must (not)</td><td rowspan="2">have a pass.
smoke.
walk on the grass.</td></tr>
<tr><td>He/She/It</td></tr>
</table>

<table>
<tr><td>I/You/We/They</td><td>do</td><td rowspan="2">not have to</td><td rowspan="2">wear a suit.
turn off the light.</td></tr>
<tr><td>He/She/It</td><td>does</td></tr>
</table>

16 Princess Diana

LAURA: Isn't she beautiful!
ROB: Who?
LAURA: Princess Diana.
ROB: Do you think so? I'm not so sure.
LAURA: I'm going to try and take some really good photos of her.
ROB: It's not that easy, you know.
LAURA: Yes, I know. But I'm still going to try.
ROB: When?
LAURA: If she opens the new hospital ward, I'll get some pictures of her there. But if that's not possible, I'll have to wait until the state opening of Parliament.
ROB: And if you can't get anything good at the opening of Parliament, what then?
LAURA: I don't know. But I'll think of something. You wait and see!

1

Look and listen. Answer the questions.

1 What does Laura think of Princess Diana?
2 What is Laura going to do?
3 What event is Laura's first choice for her photographs of the Princess?
4 What event is Laura's second choice?

Language focus

2

Helga and Pauline, from Samson's Circus, are on holiday in New York. Look at their plans for tomorrow.

3

Ask and answer, like this:

What will Helga do if it rains tomorrow?
—She'll go to the theatre.
What will she do if it's fine?
—She'll go to the zoo.

4

Ask and answer about each other, like this:

What will you do if the weather is fine tomorrow?
—I'll go for a walk in the hills.

 Helga		zoo	closed?	walk in Central Park
		theatre	closed?	cinema
 Pauline		statue of Liberty	closed?	sunbathe at the hotel
		museum of modern art	closed?	shopping

Language focus

1

Study the poster opposite.

2

Ask and answer, like this:

> What does the poster say about monkeys?
> —It says that if you're approached by monkeys, you mustn't open your car windows.

Read and write

3

Read this postcard and answer the questions.

1 Who wrote the postcard?
2 Where is Pauline?
3 When is Helga arriving at Miami airport?
4 Will Helga take a taxi?
5 Will Helga look for Pauline on the beach?

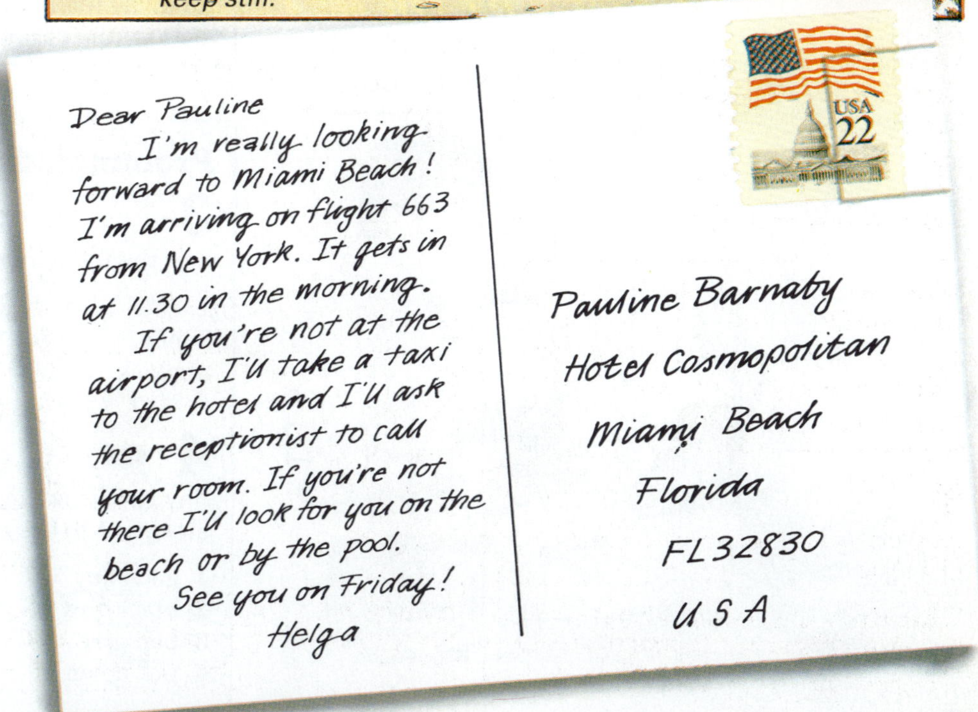

Dear Pauline

I'm really looking forward to Miami Beach! I'm arriving on flight 663 from New York. It gets in at 11.30 in the morning.

If you're not at the airport, I'll take a taxi to the hotel and I'll ask the receptionist to call your room. If you're not there I'll look for you on the beach or by the pool.

See you on Friday!

Helga

Pauline Barnaby
Hotel Cosmopolitan
Miami Beach
Florida
FL 32830
USA

4

You are going to visit a friend. You are arriving by bus or train. Write a postcard like Helga's.

16 A great party

English in use: *Speaking*

1

Look and listen.

2

Have similar conversations, like this:

problem There's so much to do. I don't know where to start.		
general offer I'll .... if you like.	*specific offer* I'll .... if you like.	
accept Thanks. Could you ......?	*accept* Thanks (a lot). That would be great.	*decline* It's all right, thanks. I can manage.
agree Sure./Of course.		

Here are some words to help you:

general	
help	
give you a hand	
specific	
take the rubbish out	do the drying up
put away the records	throw away the empty bottles
vacuum the carpet	

Pronunciation

3

Say the following words:

1 good	5 bad	9 big
2 boy	6 girl	10 dog
3 black	7 put	11 eight
4 bird	8 down	12 pence

4

Say the following words after the cassette. Pay attention to the sounds in the squares.

1 good boy	5 put back
2 blackbird	6 big dog
3 bad girl	7 eightpence
4 put down	8 goodbye

Reading

1

Read the following questions and answer them by reading the text.

1 What was wrong with the stories in French newspapers between 1958–1972?
2 What was the untrue story about Princess Diana?
3 What was the untrue story about Prince Michael of Kent's wife?
4 What was 'wrong' with the photograph of Princess Diana?

The Royal Family and the Press

Newspapers all over the world are full of stories about the British Royal Family. But are these stories accurate? Some years ago a French journalist studied the French newspapers from 1958–1972. This is what he found: the Queen (mother of four) had been pregnant 92 times. She had abdicated 63 times, had 43 'unhappy nights' and 27 nightmares.

The British newspapers are not much better, and in particular they love to print stories about Prince Charles' wife, Princess Diana. On 17th September, 1983 the *Daily Mirror* said that Diana was pregnant—twelve months before her son Harry was born!

Sometimes the stories are not so innocent. The wife of Prince Michael of Kent (one of the Queen's cousins) was, according to the press, mentally ill and had to have electric shock treatment—the story was false.

The Queen at the State Opening of Parliament with members of the Royal Family.

The Press do not only print inaccurate stories about the Royal Family; they also chase them wherever they go—like the time Charles and Diana were having a private holiday in the West Indies. While they were swimming and sunbathing two men were crawling through the undergrowth about a mile away. One of them had a large telephoto lens and took a photograph of Diana in a bikini. As soon as the photograph was published in the *Sun* newspaper the Queen complained and the newspaper had to apologize.

The Royal Family like publicity but say that the papers should tell the truth and allow them a private life. The newsmen say that the public should be told everything about the Royal Family: they are a matter for 'public concern'. It is often difficult to say who is right.

2

Answer the following questions.

1 How many children has the Queen got?
2 When was Prince Harry born?
3 According to the press, why did one of the Royal Family need electric shock treatment?
4 Which papers printed **a** the untrue story of Princess Diana's pregnancy, and **b** the photograph of the princess in a bikini?

Remember Conditionals: Type 1

General

If	the car breaks down, you are trapped in the lift,	you	should call the garage. must press the red button.

Future

If	it rains, there are any problems,	she will	go to the theatre. call for help.

17 The new tower

MAYOR: This is where the new tower will be, ladies and gentlemen, and it will provide a lot of new office space.

REPORTER: What's the timetable for the building, Mr Mayor?

MAYOR: As soon as the final plans are ready, the demolition people will move into the square. When they've cleared the site, we'll start building the new tower block. It will be finished by September and when we've moved into our new offices the building will be officially opened. I invite you all to the opening.

REPORTER: Why are you building the tower, Mr Mayor?

MAYOR: Because we need new offices.

REPORTER: But why do you have to destroy these old buildings? Why don't you convert them?

MAYOR: Progress, ladies and gentlemen, progress.

1

Look and listen. Copy these events and put the numbers 1–6 in the boxes to show the order in which they will happen.

☐ the official opening/☐ the demolition people move into the square/☐ the council move into their new offices/☐ the site is cleared/☐ the plans are ready/☐ they start building the new tower block

Language focus

2

Study the information opposite.

3

Ask and answer, like this:

> What will happen before the President's plane arrives?
> —The town officials will arrive.
> What will happen as soon as the President has walked down the steps?
> —The mayor will welcome him and introduce the town officials.

4

Ask and answer about each other, like this:

What will you do when you get home?
—I think I'll have a shower.
What then?
—After I've had a shower, I'm going to watch the football on TV.

LAWRENCE CITY COUNCIL

	PRESIDENT'S PARTY	RECEPTION COMMITTEE
10.30		Town officials arrive.
11.00	Plane arrives.	Soldiers stand to attention.
11.03	Plane engines switched off.	Town band plays.
11.04	Door opens. President appears.	Town officials walk to steps of plane.
11.06	President walks down steps.	Mayor welcomes President, introduces town officials.
11.10	President gets into car.	Mayor says goodbye. 1,000 balloons released.
11.11	President leaves airport.	Band stops playing. Town officials leave.

Language focus

1

Study the following information.
Last week the Samson family hired a yacht for a holiday. Here are some things that happened to them.

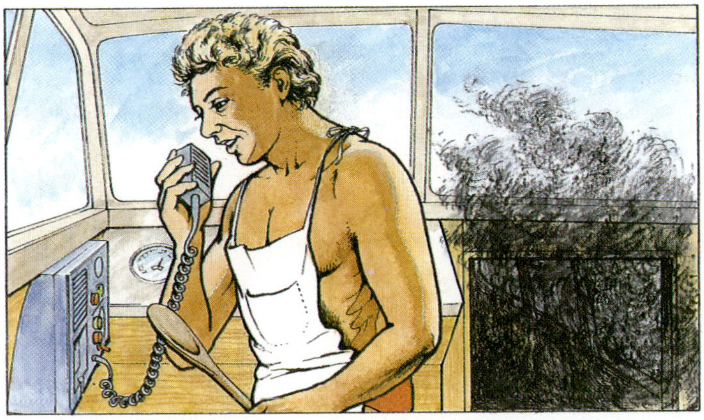

Monday David was cooking the lunch . . . the radiotelephone rang . . . David went and answered it . . . he smelt smoke and rushed back to the cooker.

Tuesday Stella was tying up the dinghy . . . Sam called to her . . . she let go of the dinghy . . . she saw it in the middle of the lagoon . . . she dived into the water and got it back.

Wednesday Daniel was sunbathing . . . it began to rain . . . he ran into the cabin and got dressed . . . he remembered his new book . . . he ran back on deck to get it.

Thursday Sam was swimming in the sea . . . Stella shouted a warning . . . Sam looked round and saw a shark . . . he swam back to the boat as quickly as possible.

2

Ask and answer, like this:

What happened while David was cooking the lunch?
—The radiotelephone rang.
What did David do when the radiotelephone rang?
—He went to answer it.
What did David do as soon as he smelt smoke?
—He rushed back to the cooker.

Read and write

3

Read the text.

While David was cooking the lunch the radiotelephone rang, so he went to answer it. While he was talking on the radiotelephone he smelt smoke, so he rushed back to the cooker. The pan was on fire.

4

Now write about Sam, Stella or Daniel in the same way, using *while*, *when*, and *so*.

17 Tea

Making the tea
Before you put in the tea, warm the pot. Then put in one teaspoonful of tea for each person and add one 'for the pot'. After you have poured in boiling water, let the tea stand for a few minutes.

Serving the tea
While you are waiting for the tea to brew, pour milk into the teacups. When the tea is ready, pour it into the cups. Add a teaspoonful of sugar if you like.

1
Answer these questions.

1 How many teaspoonfuls of tea do you put in the pot for three people?
2 What should you do after you have poured in the water?
3 Which should you pour into the cup first, the tea or the milk?

2
Use a dictionary to match the words with the pictures.

1 sprinkle	**4** pour
2 chop	**5** boil
3 stir	**6** cut

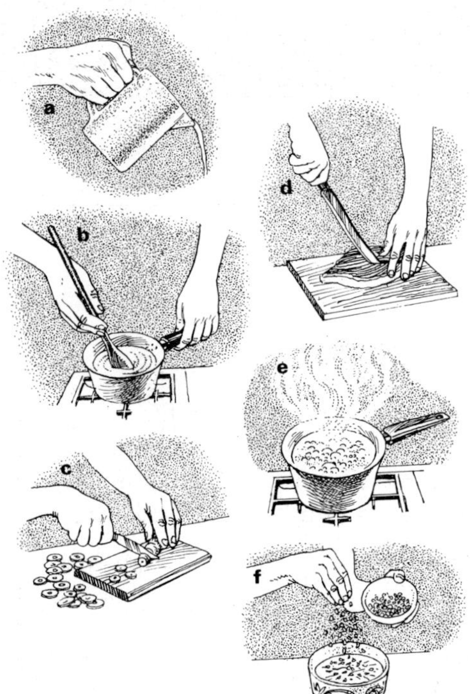

English in use: *Writing*

3
Use the words in brackets to join the following pairs of sentences.

Example: Pour in the water. Stir the mixture slowly. (after)
After you have poured in the water, stir the mixture slowly.

1 Cut the carrots into strips. Soak them in lemon juice. (*before*)
2 The onions are frying. Put some chopped garlic into the pan. (*while*)
3 Toast the bread. Sprinkle cheese onto it. (*after*)
4 Mix the salt and flour. Add the butter. (*first, then*)
5 The meal is ready. Serve it hot. (*when*)

4
Use the following instructions to write a recipe. Use *before*, *after*, *when*, *while*, *first* and *then*.

POTATO SALAD (simple)
1. Peel the potatoes. 2. Boil the potatoes. 3. Cut the boiled potatoes into small bits. 4. Leave the potatoes to cool. 5. Mix the mayonnaise. 6. Pour the mayonnaise onto the potatoes. 7. Put the potato salad into the fridge. 8. Serve the potato salad cold.

5
Write a recipe for your favourite food.
Use a dictionary if necessary.

Reading

1

Read the following statements and after reading the text, say whether they are true or false.

1 Badly designed houses waste 10% of a nation's energy.
2 The igloo is a good example of an energy-efficient house.
3 The Geohouse is energy-efficient.
4 The Geohouse is designed for a tropical rain forest.

THE GEOHOUSE *a revolution in architecture?*

Experts have estimated that badly designed houses waste 20% of a nation's energy. They let in the winter wind and the summer sun and their owners get enormous bills for gas and electricity as they try to warm their houses up—or cool them down. Clearly we must learn how to save energy in our houses.

Sometimes the simplest types of construction are the most energy-efficient. The igloo, for example, is the ideal shelter for the arctic winter. Its dome shape is perfect protection against the arctic wind, and snow is the ideal material for insulation against the cold. The pile-dwelling is ideal for the tropical rain forest. It has open sides, which provide ventilation in the hot, humid climate, and tall roofs to keep the rain away.

George Bullen, an architect, gave his 'Geohouse' many characteristics of primitive dwellings. It is heated by the sun, insulated by the earth and cooled by wind and shade. The house faces south so that solar panels catch the winter sun. In the summer, awnings are pulled out and they protect the house from the sun's direct heat. The north side of the house is semi-underground. This makes the house cool in summer and not too cold in winter because the temperature below ground seldom varies. In every way the 'Geohouse' is a design which gets its inspiration from the past.

2

Match these words with the numbers on the Geohouse:

north
south
solar panels
awnings

3

Why are the following ideal for their environments?

a the igloo
b the pile dwelling

Remember Time clauses

Before After As soon as	I/you/he/she/we/they	arrive(s) has } arrived have }	I/you/he/she/we/they	will	telephone you. start playing.

What happened	while	he was they were	cooking?

While	he was they were	talking	a friend called.

What did	he they	do	as soon as when	he heard the alarm? they got home?

18 Dinner

CARLA: What will you and I be doing in five years, I wonder?
ADRIAN: I'll probably be taking sports photographs—the same as I do now. What about you?
CARLA: The same! I'll still be working at *Quest*, I'll still be living in my flat, and I'll probably still be single.
ADRIAN: Why haven't you ever married?
CARLA: I've never found the right man, I suppose. What about you?
ADRIAN: I had a girlfriend once, but she left me.
CARLA: Do you mind being on your own?
ADRIAN: Yes, occasionally I do.
CARLA: Are you going to be on your own this evening?
ADRIAN: Yes. I'll be working on my photos for the exhibition.
CARLA: Why don't you cook me a meal instead?
ADRIAN: I'd love to, but I'm not a very good cook.
CARLA: I'm sure you are really. I'll try and come at about eight, but I might be a bit late.
ADRIAN: Come when you can. I'll give you the best meal I've ever cooked.

1

Look and listen. Answer the questions.

1 Is Carla married?
2 Has Adrian ever had a girlfriend?
3 What is Adrian going to do this evening?
4 Can Adrian cook?

Language focus

2

Study the information opposite about the activities of the President and his wife.

3

Ask and answer, like this:

> What will the President's wife be doing at three o'clock tomorrow afternoon?
> —She'll be opening a new school.
> She'll probably be making a speech.
> She might be talking to the pupils.

4

Ask and answer about each other, like this:

What will you be doing at ten o'clock tomorrow?
—I'll probably be working.

1500 hours tomorrow

	The President	The President's wife
Certain	visiting London	opening a new school
Almost certain	discussing the economic situation	making a speech
Not certain	meeting the ambassador	talking to the pupils

The high jump

Language focus

1

Look at the picture.

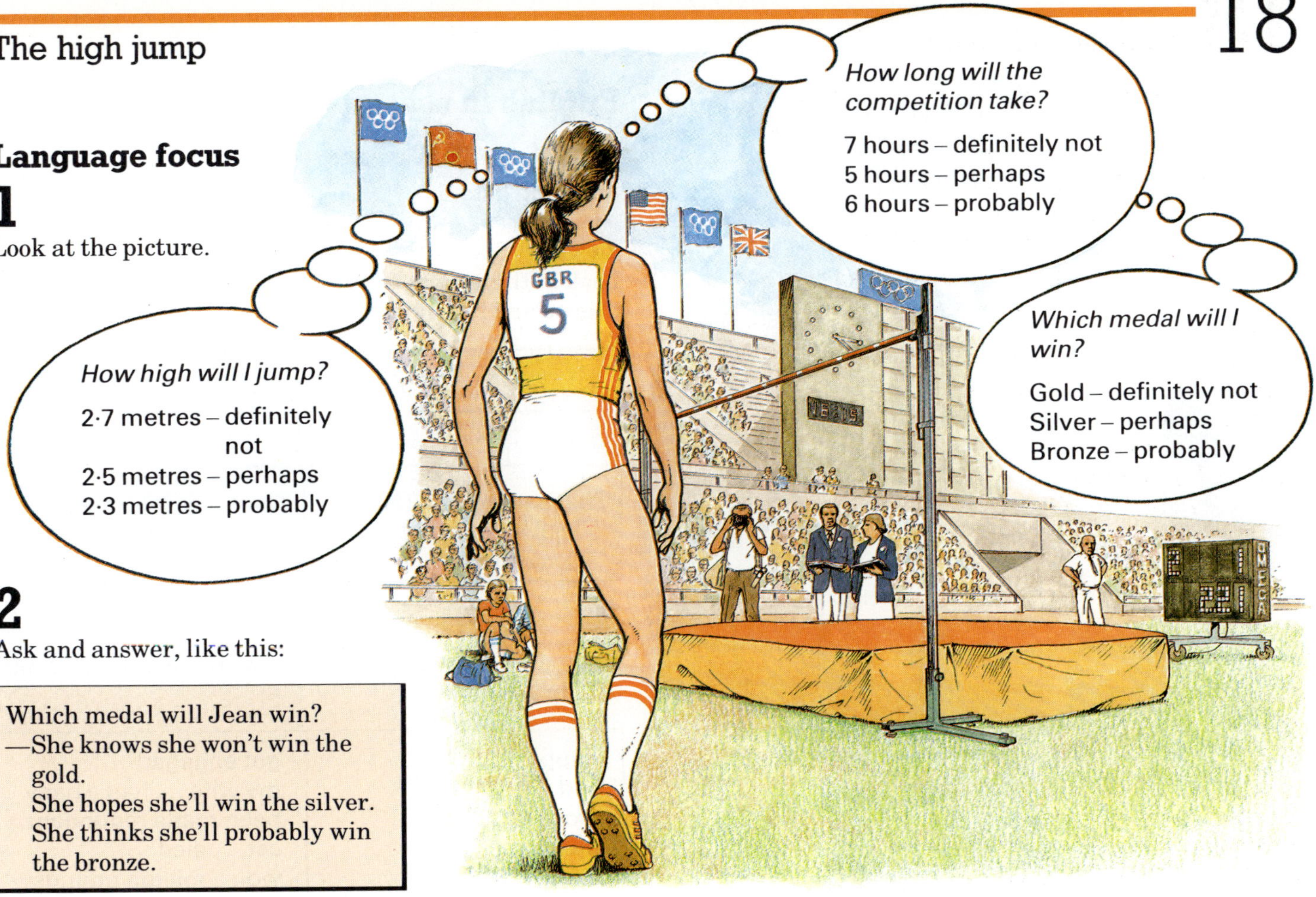

2

Ask and answer, like this:

> Which medal will Jean win?
> —She knows she won't win the gold.
> She hopes she'll win the silver.
> She thinks she'll probably win the bronze.

Read and write

3

Read this postcard and answer the questions.

1 Who wrote the postcard?
2 Where is Pauline?
3 Where is Pauline going to be
  a if the sun's shining?
  b if it's very hot?
  c if there's rain?

4

You are at a hotel and a friend is coming to see you. Write a postcard like Pauline's.

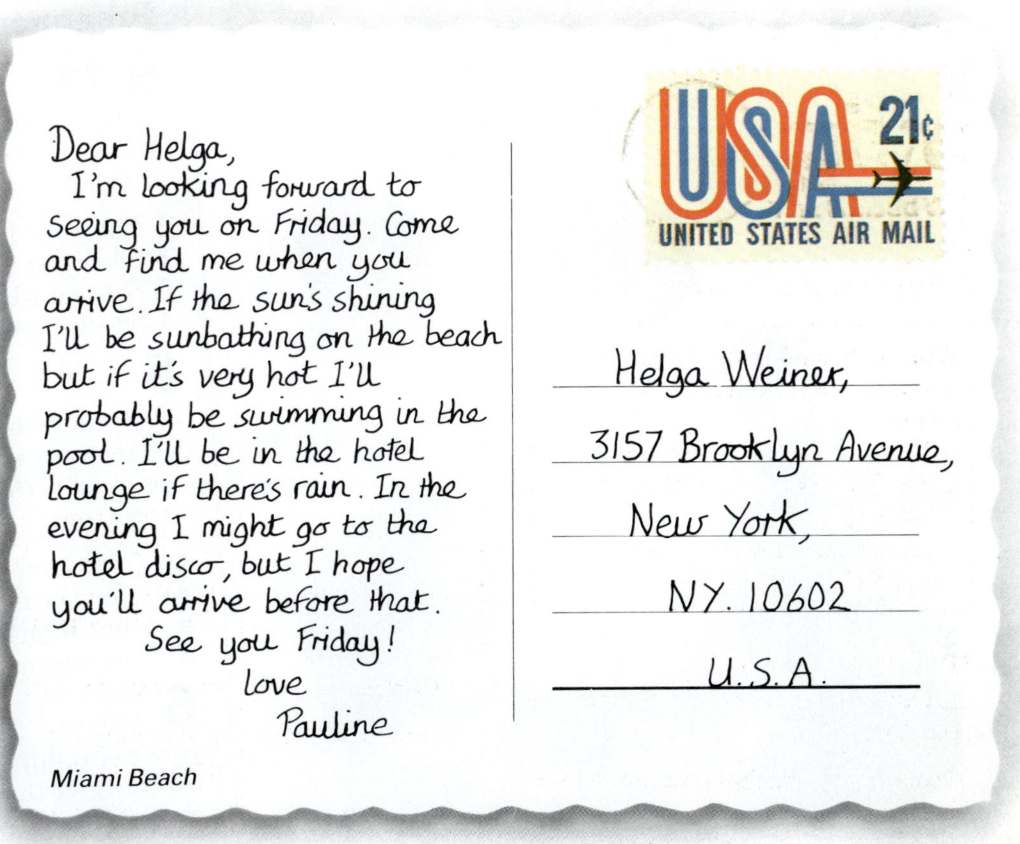

Dear Helga,
I'm looking forward to seeing you on Friday. Come and find me when you arrive. If the sun's shining I'll be sunbathing on the beach but if it's very hot I'll probably be swimming in the pool. I'll be in the hotel lounge if there's rain. In the evening I might go to the hotel disco, but I hope you'll arrive before that.
See you Friday!
love
Pauline

Helga Weiner,
3157 Brooklyn Avenue,
New York,
NY. 10602
U.S.A.

Wonderful news

English in use: *Speaking*

1

Look and listen.

2

Look at these ways of talking about or reacting to good and bad news.

You look	
I am. I've just	
That's wonderful (news)! That's fantastic! Congratulations!	That's terrible (news)! That's awful! Oh no!

3

Have similar conversations. Here are some suggestions to help you.

happy sad worried upset	got engaged my wife . . . had a baby been made redundant cat . . . died won a million pounds

Pronunciation

4

Listen to the cassette. Underline the word with the main stress in each of the sentences.

1 She won't be playing tennis.
2 She won't be playing tennis.
3 She won't be playing tennis.
4 She won't be playing tennis.

5

Now match these phrases with the sentences in exercise 4. Pay attention to the word with the main stress.

a . . . I'm sure—don't disagree with me.
b . . . but she might be playing volleyball.
c . . . but John might be playing.
d . . . but she might be watching tennis.

6

How many different meanings can you give this sentence by changing the stress?

I hope she won't buy a new car.

Reading

1

Read the following questions and answer them by reading the text.

1 Who is getting married?
2 What does the British government do every year?
3 Which of the following subjects are mentioned in the text?

marriage
leisure activities
sexual roles
illness
consumer goods
the birth rate
unemployment
home ownership

SOCIAL TRENDS

When Adrian Hutton and Carla Leone get married they will move into a new house that they have bought. But what sort of life will they have? What can they expect in modern Britain? Every year the British government publishes statistics about social trends. Their findings show definite patterns in the British way of life.

In most marriages there are some marked differences between husbands and wives. Working wives, for example, sleep (on average) one hour more every day than working husbands. Housewives, on the other hand, sleep only about three hours more every week than their working husbands. And what about housework? The government survey showed that only 1% of men do the household chores—like cleaning and ironing. But they do usually keep household accounts and it is almost always men who do repairs or improvements in the house. 30% of all marriages end in divorce.

The government survey also looked at leisure activities. They found that the two most popular leisure activities in Britain are watching television (the average family spends 20 hours a week in front of the TV set) and going for walks. Swimming is an especially popular activity among British women.

Carla and Adrian's life, though, will probably be different from the average marriage. In the first place Carla has always kept her own accounts and Adrian has always done his own housework. Neither of them like watching television very much and they both like swimming!

2

In pairs look at the information in the text and answer the following questions with one of the following: *probably*, *perhaps*, *probably not*, *no* or *I don't know*.

1 Will Adrian and Carla get divorced?
2 Will Adrian sleep more than Carla?
3 Will Adrian do the ironing?
4 Will Carla do the household accounts?
5 Will Adrian and Carla watch television at home?

Remember

Future probability

What will	I/you he/she/it we/they	be doing	at ten o'clock? in two weeks' time? on Monday morning?

I/You He/She/It We/They	will (probably) might	be	visiting Florence. watching the television. talking to the doctor.

know/think/hope

She	knows thinks hopes	he will (probably)	take three hours. win the prize. reach the top.

1 Classwork

Interaction

1

Ask other students questions to complete the chart.
Find someone who:

1 watches television every evening ....
2 has got two brothers ....
3 can play chess ....
4 is going to visit a friend tomorrow ....
5 wrote a letter last weekend ....
6 got up before 7 o'clock this morning ....
7 would like to learn Russian ....
8 cooked a meal yesterday ....
9 likes boxing ....
10 lives near a cinema ....

2

Choose one of the Bingo cards, **a**, **b**, **c** or **d**.
Listen to the teacher and cross out the verbs on your card if you hear any form of them. Shout 'Bingo' when all your squares are crossed out.

Example: You can cross out 'wait' if you hear any of these sentences: *I waited for a bus.*
We're going to wait for a bus.
I always wait for the bus, etc.

a

invent	have	stop
compose	read	put
kill	think	drive
fall	get	buy

b

miss	listen	go
love	play	cook
hate	think	visit
run	stop	watch

c

fall	read	stop
go	get	put
play	skate	open
climb	ski	type

d

buy	look	speak
cook	lift	take
sail	give	study
visit	teach	cook

Listening

Murder at Walton Hall: a radio drama in 9 parts

Part 1: Friday Night

1

Read these stories. Now listen to the cassette and say which story is the correct one.

a Sally Walton comes home with her boyfriend Bruce. She finds Anne dead in the sitting room.
b Sally Walton comes home. She talks to Anne and her mother. Anne screams. Mr Walton is dead.
c Sally Walton comes home. She talks to Anne and then to her father. Anne screams. Mrs Walton is dead.

2

Listen to the cassette and fill in the blanks.

SALLY: Hello, Daddy. ....?
MR WALTON: I'm not feeling very well, actually. But I'll be all right in the morning. What about you? .... the show?
SALLY: Oh Yes! I thought it was fantastic. All the .... and .... were on roller skates and they were –
MR WALTON: .... did you go ....?
SALLY: Er, with Bruce.
MR WALTON: Ah, Bruce.
SALLY: .... with me?
MR WALTON: Look, Sally, you're an .... You're nearly 21 years old!
SALLY: But what about Mummy?
MR WALTON: Your mother .... Bruce, and frankly I can't say –

Interaction

1:

Student **A**: Look at number 1 on page 95. Ask **B** questions to complete this chart about Bruno Marini. Answer **B**'s questions about Ricardo Lopes.
Student **B**: Look at number 1 on page 98. Ask **A** questions to complete this chart about Ricardo Lopes. Answer **A**'s questions about Bruno Marini.
Do not look at each other's pages until you have finished.

NAME: ....

MARRIED/SINGLE: .... *CHILDREN:* ....

SPORT: ....

INTERESTS: ....

Question	***no***	***yes***	***when?***
been married?	.....	.....	....
won a race?	.....	.....	....
broken a record?	.....	.....	....
had any accidents?	.....	.....	....

Now discuss this question.
Who would you like to meet, Ricardo or Bruno? Why?

2:

Complete the following passage about the student next to you by asking questions. Delete words that you don't need.

My neighbour is a ...., and her/his name is .... Her/His home is in ...., in ....

She/He started to learn English .... ago.

Her/His favourite .... is ...., but she/he likes .... too.

My neighbour has never ...., and she/he has never ...., but she/he has ....

My neighbour is going to .... next .... and she/he would like to ....

Listening

Murder at Walton Hall: a radio drama in 9 parts

The story so far . . . *Sally Walton arrived home after an evening at the theatre with her boyfriend, Bruce Carter. The maid, Anne, screamed when she found Mrs Walton – dead.*

Part 2: The Next Morning

1

Read these statements and then listen to the cassette. Say whether they are true or false.

1. Inspector Wade goes to Walton Hall with Sergeant Pride.
2. Mr Walton is at home.
3. The murderer used a knife.
4. Bruce Carter, Sally's boyfriend, is at Walton Hall.
5. Sally Walton prepares the evening meal every day.

2

Student **A** is at home. No one from **A**'s family is at home. Student **B** is a detective. **B** must find out where all the other members of **A**'s family are, when they went out, etc.

Interaction

1:

Look at number 9 on page 101. **A** gives **B** directions. **B** follows the directions on the map and finds out where they take him (without looking at **A**).

2:

Match the words with the numbers in the picture.

top shelf
bottom shelf
table
fridge
drawer
stool
chair

Use the words below to give your partner instructions, like this: *"Draw three cups on the table. Draw the milk in the fridge."* Use the big picture on page 104 for your drawing. Write down each instruction as you give it.

Listening

Murder at Walton Hall: a radio drama in 9 parts

The story so far... *Inspector Wade and Sergeant Pride have visited Walton Hall to ask questions about the murder of Mrs Walton. Mrs Walton was poisoned. Bruce Carter, Sally Walton's boyfriend, has accused Anne, the maid, of Mrs Walton's murder.*

Part 3: A Telephone Call

1

Study the map. Now listen to the cassette and put a cross (X) where you think Stan's house is.

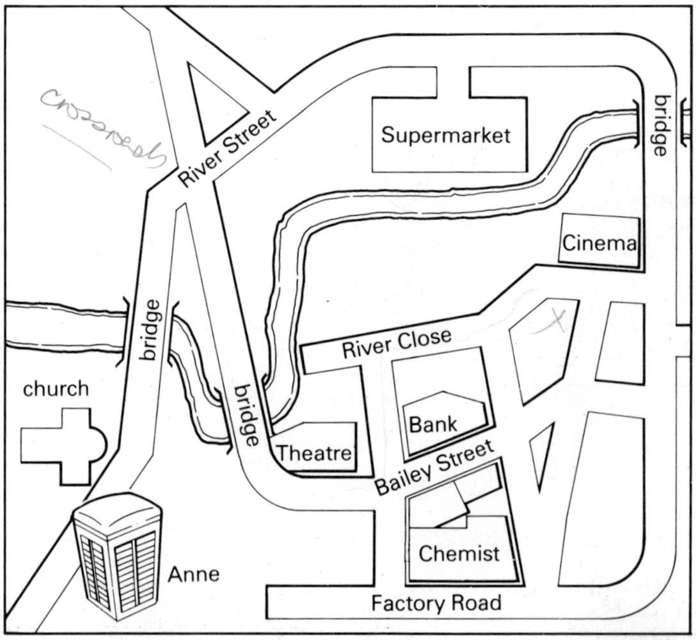

2

Using the map in exercise 1 have phone conversations in which student **A** rings up student **B** and asks for directions. Mark **B**'s house on the map.

Interaction

1 ∴∴

Team **A**: use this symbol, **0** (nought).
Team **B**: use this symbol, **X** (cross).

1. A member of Team **A** chooses a square.
2. He or she then makes a sentence or question with the word in that square.
3. If it is correct, a **0** is put on that square.
4. Team **B** do the same with a different square and put a **X** if they make a correct sentence.
5. The first team with a straight line of noughts or crosses wins.

a

enough	some	ago
just	just	always
any	turning	too

b

suntanned	too	receiver
parachute	enough	button
newsagent's	just	meet

2 :

In pairs, decide what the people are saying.

Listening

Murder at Walton Hall: a radio drama in 9 parts

The story so far . . . *Anne, the maid at Walton Hall, was very frightened because of Mrs Walton's murder. She wanted to talk to her friend Stan, the gardener at Walton Hall. But she never arrived at his house.*

Part 4: Coffee

1

Read columns **A** and **B**. Listen to the cassette and match the names in column **A** with column **B**.

1 Mr Walton	**a** was with Sally at the theatre on the night of Mrs Walton's murder.
2 Sally Walton	**b** is the gardener at Walton Hall.
3 Anne Clarke	**c** doesn't know where Mr Walton is.
4 Stan	**d** thinks she has seen Bruce before.
5 Bruce Carter	**e** is Sally's sister.
6 Inspector Wade	**f** probably didn't murder Mrs Walton, according to Inspector Wade.
7 Vanessa	**g** has disappeared.

2

Listen to the cassette and fill in the blanks.

WADE: The heater in this car .... I'm freezing.

PRIDE: Me ...., Inspector. Shall we stop .... have .... coffee?

WADE: Yes, John. That's a ....

PRIDE: Well, Inspector, ... who poisoned Mrs Walton?

WADE: Not yet, not yet, John. .... too many questions and not .... answers.

PRIDE: What about the husband, Mr Walton?

WADE: Yes, I'm interested in Mr Walton. .... – even Sally Walton doesn't know where he is.

Interaction

1

Ask other students questions to complete the chart.

FIND SOMEONE WHO

1 was given a good present for their last birthday

....

2 has just received some good news

....

3 was invited to a party last week

....

4 always sends their brother a card on his birthday

....

5 was taken to the theatre last year

....

6 has never been to a discotheque

....

7 has just read an interesting book

....

2

In pairs, look at the picture and number the cards in the correct order to make a dialogue. The first one is done for you.

- Hello, Julia. You look happy!
- Who by?
- Is it a lot?
- Yes! Yes, I would. Thanks very much.
- I am. I've just been given some money.
- No, just about enough for a good meal for two. Would you like to come and eat?
- Oh, no! But she wanted me to have the money.
- Has she died?
- An old aunt of mine.

3

You have just been given £50 by your grandmother. With your partner decide how to spend it and write a dialogue like the one above.

Listening

Murder at Walton Hall: a radio drama in 9 parts

The story so far . . . *The police want to know who killed Mrs Walton. Was it Mr Walton – who has disappeared? How is Bruce Carter mixed up in all this? What is Vanessa Walton's relationship with her family? Inspector Wade and Sergeant Pride have just heard the news about Anne Clarke, the maid at Walton Hall – she was murdered too.*

Part 5: Vanessa

1

Read the questions. Choose the correct answer by listening to the cassette.

1 When Vanessa sees the police she is
- **a** happy. ☐
- **b** enthusiastic. ☐
- **c** unenthusiastic. ☐

2 Vanessa lives in
- **a** a big luxurious house. ☐
- **b** a dirty little house. ☐
- **c** a nice modern house. ☐

3 Vanessa spent her money on
- **a** drugs. ☐
- **b** clothes. ☐
- **c** holidays. ☐

4 Vanessa went to Walton Hall
- **a** last Friday. ☐
- **b** three weeks ago. ☐
- **c** three days ago. ☐

2

Look at these two lines from Part 5 of *Murder at Walton Hall*.

VANESSA: I've spent my money. I haven't got any left.
PRIDE: What did you spend it on, Miss Walton? Clothes? Food? Holidays?

In groups (and then with the whole class) find out what people usually spend their money on.

6 Classwork

Interaction

How did you come to school today?
By bus
Why?
Because ---

1:

Student **A**: look at number 2 on page 95. Complete the chart by asking **B** questions.
Student **B**: look at number 2 on page 98. Complete the chart by asking **A** questions.
Do not look at each other's charts until you have finished.

2:

Ask your neighbour about things he or she wanted to do but didn't.

A: *I wanted to go to the film at the ABC last night.*
B: *Why didn't you?*
A: *Because I had too much homework.*

3:

In groups look at the pictures. Choose any three of them and tell a story which connects them.

Listening

Murder at Walton Hall: a radio drama in 9 parts

The story so far... *After the murders of Mrs Walton and Anne Clarke, Inspector Wade and Sergeant Pride went to see Vanessa Walton. Inspector Wade discovered that Vanessa is a drug addict.*

Part 6: Stan The Gardener

1

Read the following questions and answer them by listening to the cassette.

1 Who goes to see Stan?
2 How long has Stan worked at Walton Hall?
3 Who did Anne see in the garden on the day before Mrs Walton's death?
4 What were the two people doing in the garden?
5 What does Inspector Wade know about Bruce Carter?

2

Listen to the cassette and fill in the blanks.

PRIDE: My name's Sergeant Pride. .... I .... a word with you?

STAN: It's about the ...., is it?

PRIDE: Yes.

STAN: .... come in. I'll just .... the television.

PRIDE: Now, Mr Williams, you work as a .... at Walton Hall?

STAN: Yes.

PRIDE: And .... have you worked there?

STAN: For five years.

PRIDE: What about ....?

STAN: She's been here – she came to Walton Hall .... months ....

Interaction

1

Student **A**: Look at number 3 on page 95. Find out from **B** which square each picture goes in. Write the number in the square.
Student **B**: Look at number 3 on page 98. Help **A** by giving information about the position of your pictures. ***Do not say any numbers.*** *Do not look at your partner's page until you have finished.*

2

Fill in the first column with the names of foods. Ask people if they like the foods. Record their answers with a tick (√) for yes and a cross (×) for no. Write their reason for liking or disliking the food (e.g. *It tastes horrible*) in the 'Reasons' column. An example has been given.

Name of food	*Yes/No*	*Reasons*
snails	X	They taste horrible.

Listening

Murder at Walton Hall: a radio drama in 9 parts

The story so far . . . *Stan Williams, the gardener at Walton Hall, has told Sergeant Pride about the meeting between Vanessa Williams and the chemist, Mr Burton. Inspector Wade has discovered that Bruce Carter was once in prison because he sold drugs.*

Part 7: At The Chemist's

1

Read these statements and then listen to the cassette. Say which are correct.

1 Mr Burton goes to see the police.
2 Mr Burton was a witness for Mr Walton's new will.
3 Mr Burton didn't meet Vanessa at Walton Hall.
4 Mr Burton doesn't want to tell the police about the will or about Vanessa.
5 Mr Walton is at Mr Burton's shop.

2

Listen to the cassette and fill in the blanks.

ASSISTANT: Good morning. .... I .... you?
PRIDE: Er . . . yes, please. .... to speak to Mr Burton, if that's possible.
ASSISTANT: If you just wait a minute, I'll go .... get him.
PRIDE: Thank you.
WADE: What .... you .... there, Sergeant?
PRIDE: I don't know. It says 'moisturizing cream'.
WADE: Ugh – it looks ....
PRIDE: Yes. But it .... OK.
BURTON: .... you?
WADE: Yes, Mr Burton, I think you can.
BURTON: I'm sorry?
WADE: We're police officers, Mr Burton.

Interaction

1 :::

1 Write an adjective in each section of the Meridian Wheel.
2 Divide into two teams.
3 Someone from team **A** chooses a number from 1–12.
4 Someone from team **B** says his adjective for that number.
5 The member from team **A** uses that adjective to compare two things, e.g.

old – *My father is older than my mother.*

6 If the member from team **A** is correct (without help) team **A** get two points. If the member from team **A** is helped by the rest of the team, then team **A** get one point.

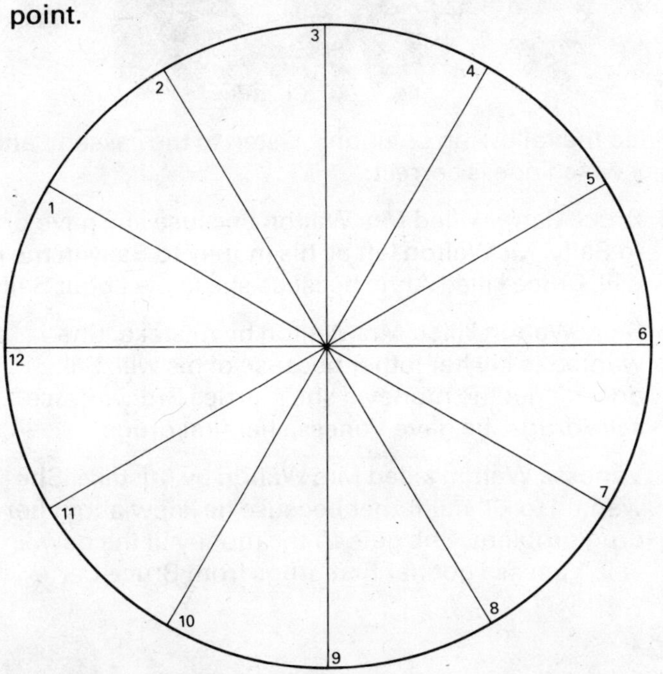

2 :

Student **A**: look at number 4 on page 96. Find the differences between your picture and **B**'s by asking **B**.
Student **B**: look at number 4 on page 99. Find the differences between your picture and **A**'s by asking **A**.
Do not look at each other's pictures until you have finished.

Listening

Murder at Walton Hall: a radio drama in 9 parts

The story so far... *Inspector Wade and Sergeant Pride have talked to Mr Burton, the chemist. He told them about Mr Walton's new will and they asked him about his meeting with Vanessa. They met Mr Walton for the first time.*

Part 8: Mr Walton's Story

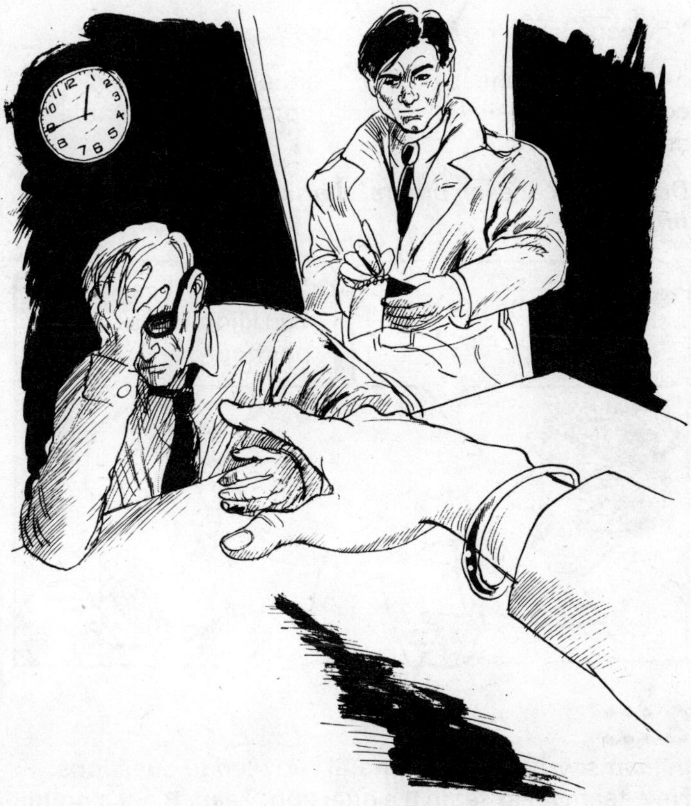

1

Read the questions and then answer *yes* or *no* by listening to the cassette.

1 Does Mr Walton usually eat margarine?
2 Did Mr Walton eat any toast on the evening of his wife's murder?
3 Does Mr Walton have a problem with his heart?
4 Did Mrs Walton have butter with her toast on the night of her death?
5 Does Inspector Wade know the name of the murderer?

2

You are making your will. You are going to leave all your money to some organisations, e.g. a museum, a home for elderly people, a sports organisation, an international famine relief agency.

- Write down the name of three organisations.
- Get in pairs. Try to agree on your lists of three organisations.
- Get in groups of four. Try to agree about your lists.

Interaction

1

Student **A**: Look at number 5 on page 96. Complete your chart by asking **B** and **C** questions.
Student **B**: Look at number 5 on page 99. Complete your chart by asking **A** and **C** questions.
Student **C**: Look at number 5 on page 105. Complete your chart by asking **A** and **B** questions.

You can use some or all of these words:

expensive cheap big small fast economical reliable quiet comfortable stable attractive

Do not look at each others' charts until you have finished.

2

In teams write twenty general knowledge questions. Now team **A** ask team **B** a question. Team **B** get a point if they can answer correctly. Then team **B** ask team **A** a question. The team with the most points wins the game.

Listening

Murder at Walton Hall: a radio drama in 9 parts

The story so far... *Detective Inspector Wade knows who the murderer is. She knows that Mrs Walton died because she ate her husband's margarine. And she now knows the details of Mr Walton's new will.*

Part 9: The Arrest

1

Read the following solutions. Listen to the cassette and say which one is correct.

a Bruce Carter killed Mrs Walton because she gave drugs to Sally. Mr Walton left all his money to Sally in the new will. Bruce killed Anne because she knew about Sally.

b Sally Walton killed Mrs Walton by mistake. She wanted to kill her father because of his will. Sally doesn't get the money if she marries Bruce. Bruce sells drugs; he gave Vanessa her first drugs.

c Vanessa Walton killed Mrs Walton by mistake. She wanted to kill her father because he knew about her drug problem. She gets all the money in the new will. Vanessa got her first drugs from Bruce Carter.

2

Listen to the cassette and fill in the blanks.

WADE: Mr Carter, which is ...., heroin or cocaine?

CARTER: Well it depends on the quality, but –

PRIDE: You're quite an expert, ..., Mr Carter?

SALLY: Leave my boyfriend ...., Sergeant Pride.

PRIDE: In a minute, Miss Walton. When .... meet Vanessa, Mr Carter?

CARTER: About two years ago.

WADE: And you sold her drugs. You gave her heroin, ...?

CARTER: I . . . er . . .

Interaction

1 : :

Look at the picture and then number the cards in the correct order to make a dialogue.

- 1 Have I shown you this photo of me?
- That's fantastic! It's the biggest fish I've ever seen! What did you do with it?
- I don't believe you!
- It's a pike.
- It's true.
- A pike! Where did you get it?
- I put it back in the river.
- No. What are you holding?
- I caught it.

2 : :

In England some people do not like hunting, shooting or fishing. They want to stop these sports. Do you agree with them?

3 : :

Meridian Trail:
a game for 3–5 players

Meridian Trail

You need:
* a dice
* the Trail board on page 102–103
* a small piece of paper with your name on it to use as a 'counter'

How to play

1. Throw the dice. The player with the top score starts the game.
2. The player throws the dice. If, for example, the dice shows 4, he goes forward four squares.
3. If a player lands on, for example, a *GO TO 6* square, he goes forward to square number 6. If he lands on a *GO BACK TO 3* square, he goes back to square number 3.
4. When a player lands on a *RISK* square, all the players must look at the *RISK* questions on page 75. For unit 10 the player must choose the number between 1 and 10 on the *RISK* square and answer the question. If the other players say 'correct', he goes forward one square. If they say 'wrong', he goes back one square. If in doubt, ask the teacher.
5. The winner is the first player at number 30.

Listening

The Air Taxi Mystery: a radio drama in 9 parts

Part 1: The Crash

1

Read the following stories. Listen to the cassette and say which one is the correct story.

a Inspector Wade is in an aeroplane with her husband. The plane crashes into a field but Sheila Wade is not hurt. Tony, her husband, is killed.

b A pilot is in trouble and he calls air traffic control. The plane crashes into the sea next to Sheila and Tony Wade's boat.

c A pilot is in trouble and she calls air traffic control. The plane crashes in Cornwall, where Sheila and Tony Wade are in their holiday cottage.

2

Fuel pipe Padstow Negative too much cloud

In groups of three fill in the following chart about the holidays you all take.

NAME:			
FAVOURITE HOLIDAY ACTIVITIES:			
FAVOURITE PLACE(S) FOR HOLIDAYS:			
FREQUENCY OF HOLIDAYS:			

Compare your results with other groups.

Interaction

1

In groups of four, students **A** and **B** fill in the chart about each other. Students **C** and **D** fill in the chart about each other.

NAME:	THE LAST TIME:
eat an egg	2 days ago.
travel by taxi	last night
meet an interesting person	4 days ago
read a good book	2 days ago
write a letter	2 weeks ago
sing a song	—
ride a bicycle	3 years ago
receive a postcard	in the last holidays

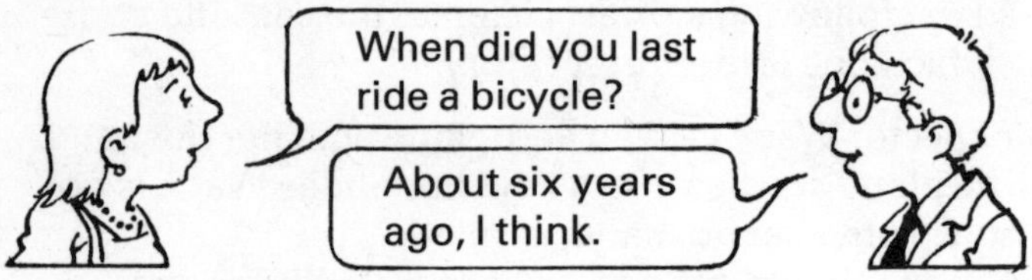

Now **A** joins **C**, and **B** joins **D**. **A** tells **C** about **B**, and **C** tells **A** about **D**, and so on.

2

Complete the following chart about films/TV programmes by asking your colleagues what is the most interesting film/TV programme they've ever seen, etc.

	Names of films/TV programmes
most interesting	
most frightening	
most moving	
most boring	
funniest	

In groups compare results.

Listening

The Air Taxi Mystery: a radio drama in 9 parts

The story so far... *Detective Inspector Wade has gone to her holiday cottage in Cornwall with her husband, Tony. After supper they were talking when they heard an aeroplane. It crashed.*

Part 2: The Constable's Story

1

Read the following statements and then listen to the cassette and say which are correct.

1 The crashing plane missed Sheila and Tony's house.
2 The crashing plane hit Sheila and Tony's house.
3 Inspector Wade has a conversation with the pilot.
4 Inspector Wade talks to a policeman.
5 The pilot was a man.
6 The pilot was a woman.
7 The door of the crashed plane was open.
8 The door of the crashed plane was shut.

2

In groups:
* Have interviews with Sheila and Tony Wade about the crash.
* Make notes of the facts that you know about the crash.
* Write a report of the crash for the local newspaper.

12 Classwork

Interaction

1

Complete the following chart by questioning other students.

Find someone who:

1 was watching TV at 8 p.m. last night

....

2 hasn't had a cup of coffee since last Sunday

....

3 wasn't sleeping at 3 a.m. this morning

....

4 is going to leave the country next month

....

5 has never seen a film with Robert Redford

....

6 was doing their homework at 7 p.m. last Sunday

....

7 has just bought something very expensive

....

8 wasn't having breakfast at 7.30 a.m. this morning

....

2

In groups look at the pictures. Choose any three of them and tell a story which connects them.

Listening

The Air Taxi Mystery: a radio drama in 9 parts

The story so far ... *Detective Inspector Wade was on holiday with her husband. A plane crashed near her house and she talked to the local police about it. She now knows that the door of the plane was open when it crashed.*

Part 3: The Chief Investigator

1

Read the following questions and answer them by listening to the cassette.

1 What time did the plane crash, according to Inspector Wade?
2 Who does Inspector Wade see at the Aviation Accident Board?
3 What time did the plane's radio stop?

2

Listen to the cassette and fill in the blanks.

PRIDE: Did you enjoy your weekend, Inspector?

WADE: No, John, I did not! I .... nearly .... by a Cessna Citation!

PRIDE: Ah! ....?

WADE: A Cessna Citation. It's a type of aeroplane, Sergeant.

PRIDE: ....?

WADE: It was about quarter past ten in the evening. We were .... in the dining room of our house after a delicious supper. We ...., when suddenly we heard this screaming engine and a plane smashed into the field .... the house.

PRIDE: But you weren't hurt, Inspector!

WADE: No, we were .... Of course the pilot was killed – a woman, I understand. But .... one or two things about the crash that puzzle me.

Interaction

1 :

In pairs use phrases from box **A** to make sentences with phrases from box **B**. You can make any sentences you want!

A	B
I was singing	the police arrived
she was dancing	he fell off his chair
they were laughing	she tripped over a chair
he was reading	the lights went out
they were sleeping	the aeroplane crashed
she was having a bath	her ex-husband arrived
I was talking to my mother	the bank was robbed
we were playing chess	the volcano erupted
I was writing a letter	the children started crying

Now complete phrases from *either* box **A** or box **B** to make sentences of your own.

2 : :

In groups look at the following advertisement for a job with a security firm. Decide which of the four applicants should get the job.

The successful candidate should be between 25–40 with a Secondary school certificate. Male candidates should be between 1.65 m and 1.85 m and female candidates should be between 1.60 m and 1.75 m. Candidates should have good eyesight and be fit and healthy.

Name: James Conan
Age: 24
Height: 1.60m
Health: fairly good
Eyesight: quite good
Qualifications: Secondary school certificate

Name: Caroline White
Age: 41
Height: 1.78m
Health: good
Eyesight: excellent
Qualifications: University doctorate

Name: Shirley Grey
Age: 26
Height: 1.65 m
Health: excellent
Eyesight: poor
Qualifications: University degree

Name: Paul Green
Age: 28
Height: 1.87m
Health: excellent
Eyesight: good
Qualifications: Primary school certificate

Example: **A**: I think James Conan should get the job.
B: I don't agree. He's too short and he isn't old enough.

Listening

The Air Taxi Mystery: a radio drama in 9 parts

The story so far... *Detective Inspector Wade was asked to go to the Aviation Accident Board. There she listened to a tape of the aeroplane crash. She told the Chief Investigator that the pilot was murdered.*

Part 4: The Cutter Air Taxi Service

1

Read the names in column **A** and the words in column **B**. Match them by listening to the cassette.

1 Glenda — **a** is the mechanic.
2 Sarah — **b** is the business manager.
3 Brian — **c** is the owner of the air taxi service.
4 Glenda — **d** is a pilot.
5 Barry — **e** is Sarah's sister-in-law.

1d/e 2c 3b 4d/e 5a

2

Listen to the cassette and fill in the blanks.

BRIAN: It's a bad morning for you, ...?

SARAH: Well, yes. Yes, it is. .... Robert, ... Rose.

BRIAN: There's no connection. Rose had engine failure. She was flying along quite happily and then her .... cut out.

SARAH: But why? The plane .... a complete service the day before.

BRIAN: I know. I .... it either.

SARAH: Where's Glenda?

BRIAN: Oh, yes. She .... me .... give you a message. She's .... upset .... come in today.

SARAH: Well, so am I, but I'm here.

14 Classwork

Interaction

1 ••

In pairs look at the picture and number the cards in the correct order to make a dialogue. The first one is done for you.

- *1* Mrs Carr, what happened here tonight?
- Did you see the crash?
- I rushed out. I heard a baby. It was crying, so I ran towards it and pulled it from the fire. It was taken away by the ambulancemen.
- A small plane crashed in a field outside the house.
- I was washing my hair.
- I'm sure you did. What were you doing when you heard the plane?
- Oh, no. But I heard it.
- You're a very brave woman, Mrs Carr.
- And what did you do?

2 •••

Group **A**: Look at number 6 on page 97.
Group **B**: Look at number 6 on page 100.
Group **C**: Look at number 6 on page 105.
Group **D**: Look at number 6 on page 106.
Each group writes two sentences (in the past) about their picture.

Then make new groups of four with one person from groups **A**, **B**, **C** and **D**. Tell the story in sequence *without looking at the pictures.*

Listening

The Air Taxi Mystery: a radio drama in 9 parts

The story so far... *Inspector Wade thinks that Rose Melville was murdered. Rose was a pilot for the Cutter Air Taxi Service and Inspector Wade went to meet the owner, Sarah Cutter. Inspector Wade reminded Mrs Cutter of her husband's death six months earlier.*

Part 5: Robert Cutter's Story

1

Read these paragraphs. Now listen to the cassette and say which one is correct.

a Wade and Pride go to talk to Robert Cutter. He tells them that he nearly died in a car crash. His wife wanted the air taxi company and tried to kill him.

b The Chief Investigator tells Wade and Pride that Robert Cutter flew over the sea and ran out of fuel. A boat found a part of his aeroplane.

c The Chief Investigator plays Wade and Pride a tape of Robert Cutter in his aeroplane. He is shouting about engine failure and he crashes into the sea.

2

Listen to the cassette and fill in the blanks.

SECRETARY: Good morning, ...?

WADE: Yes, please. I'd like to .... the Chief Investigator.

SECRETARY: Can I have your name, please?

WADE: Yes, certainly. I'm Detective .... and this is ....

SECRETARY: Well, if you .... here, I'll .... and see if he's free.

PRIDE: I .... Mr Mason will see us.

WADE: Of course ....

15 Classwork

Interaction

1

1 Write a word in each section of the Meridian Wheel.
2 Divide into two teams.
3 Someone from team **A** chooses a number from 1–12.
4 Someone from team **B** says his word for that number.
5 Someone from team **A** uses that word to make a sentence or a question.
6 If the member from team **A** is correct (without help), team **A** get two points. If the member from team **A** is helped by one of the team, then team **A** get one point.

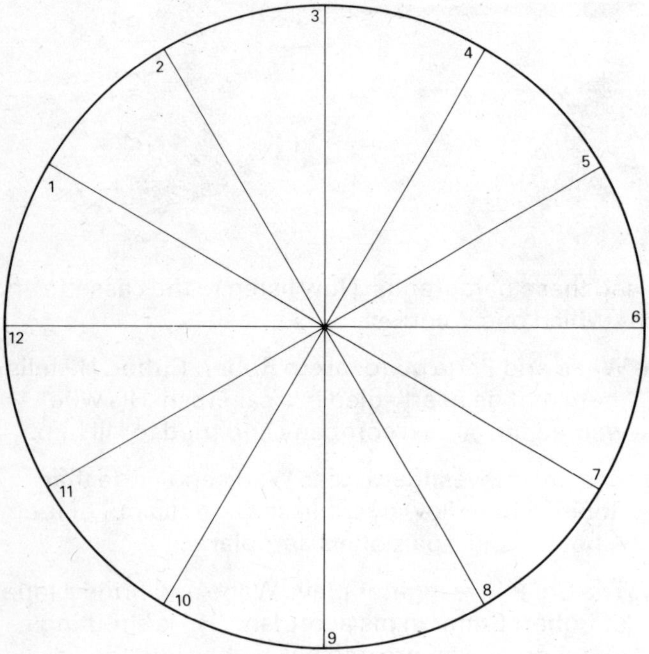

2

Student **A**: Look at number 7 on page 97. Find out about the Naseby Culture Club by asking **B** questions.
Student **B**: Look at number 7 on page 100. Find out about the Chesholt Culture Club by asking **A** questions.

Write a short description of the club you have found out about.

Listening

The Air Taxi Mystery: a radio drama in 9 parts

The story so far... *Inspector Wade wanted to know more about Robert Cutter's death, so she went to see the Chief Investigator at the Aviation Accident Board. The Chief Investigator told Wade about Robert Cutter's death six months earlier; he flew out to sea and disappeared.*

Part 6: Barry

1

Read the following statements and then listen to the cassette. Say which statements are correct.

1 Barry is in the hangar.
2 Barry is in the office.
3 Sarah has three brothers.
4 Sarah has one brother.
5 Barry gave Rose's plane a service the week before her crash.
6 Barry gave Rose's plane a service the day before her crash.
7 Barry is unhappy because Glenda arrives.
8 Barry is happy because Glenda arrives.

2

- Imagine that you have an unusual occupation (lion-tamer, kite-maker, wine-taster, etc.).
- In groups, interview each other about these occupations. Find out what people do, what they like about their job, what they have to do, etc.
- Choose one of the interviews and write a newspaper article about it.

16 Classwork

Interaction

1 :

In pairs use phrases from box **A** to make sentences with phrases from box **B**. You can make any sentence you want!

A
If it rains,
If he arrives late,
If she doesn't ring soon,
If I find the right man,
If we finish this exercise,
If I can afford it,
If I feel energetic,
If you go to cookery classes,
If I find the right woman,

B
I'll get married
I'll dance the tango
I'll have a swim
I'll go to Australia
I'll get fatter
I'll scream
I'll buy a new jacket
I'll tell him to go away
I'll watch TV for six hours

2 : :

In groups try to find the solutions to the following problems.

a

You are being chased by a gang of robbers. The road forks into two. There is a man standing at each fork. You have been told that one man always tells the truth. His road leads to a friendly village. The other man always tells a lie and his road leads to a dangerous village. What one question can you ask to make sure that you get to the friendly village?

b

In the middle of a desert you find a large building with one small door. There is a lorry outside the door. In the building there is a dead man hanging from a rope. On the ground there is a pool of water. What has happened?

Listening

The Air Taxi Mystery: a radio drama in 9 parts

The story so far... *Inspector Wade is investigating the death of the pilot Rose Melville (and the earlier death of Robert Cutter). She has discovered that Sarah Cutter does not have any relations except for her brother, Barry. Sergeant Pride talked to Barry, the mechanic.*

Part 7: Glenda

1

Read the following questions and then answer *yes* or *no* by listening to the cassette.

1 Has Glenda got a trophy for winning a parachuting championship?
2 Has Glenda worked for the Cutter Air Taxi Service for more than two years?
3 Does Glenda like flying?
4 Does Glenda like Barry?
5 Was Sarah very upset when her husband died, according to Glenda?
6 Did Sarah always want to be the boss of the Air Taxi Service, according to Glenda?

2

Listen to the cassette and fill in the blanks.

GLENDA: Oh, hello.

WADE: Good morning, Mrs Neal. .... your husband .... ?

GLENDA: No, he's gone to the office.

WADE: .... you .... today?

GLENDA: Yes, I'm am later. .... to Scotland this afternoon.

WADE: Oh, ... are you going .... ?

GLENDA: I'm taking some tourists to see Edinburgh.

WADE: It's a .... city.

GLENDA: If you say so. Now then, ... you .... some coffee?

17 Classwork

Interaction

1:

In pairs look at the picture and number the sentences in the correct order to make a dialogue. The first one is done for you.

1 What do you want me to do today?

3 OK. What time will it take place?

5 Who's going to open the bridge?

7 Really? And what's the programme?

4 Well, the ceremony starts at midday.

9 And is that all?

6 The Minister of Transport.

2 We'd like you to film the opening of the new bridge over the River Bere.

10 Oh, no. As soon as the ribbon's been cut, he'll drive across the bridge with the mayor.

8 Well, after he's made a speech, the Minister will cut the ribbon.

11 OK, then. I'd better get going.

2:

In pairs write a speech for the opening of a new school or hospital.

3:

In groups look at the pictures. Tell a story which connects them in some way.

Listening

The Air Taxi Mystery: a radio drama in 9 parts

The story so far... *Inspector Wade has talked to Glenda and looked at her parachuting trophy. Glenda thinks that Sarah always wanted to be the boss of Cutter Air Taxis and was not very upset when Robert Cutter died.*

Part 8: Waiting

1

Read the following questions and answer them by listening to the cassette.

1 What is Sarah going to do, according to Barry?
2 When is Sarah going to do it, according to Barry?
3 What doesn't Sarah want?
4 Why might a pilot open the door of a crashing plane?
5 What are Brian, Sarah, and the policemen going to do?

2

Listen to the cassette and fill in the blanks.

BARRY: What .... you .... this time?

PRIDE: .... just .... a few questions.

BARRY: All right.

PRIDE: .... outside?

BARRY: OK. But please make it quick. .... I've finished working on that plane, I've got to give .... plane a service.

PRIDE: Oh, really? Is she going to use it?

BARRY: Yes. She .... get away, she says. She's going to .... tomorrow morning.

PRIDE: Oh, is she? Now then, Barry, when .... you last .... Rose?

18 Classwork

Interaction

1

Student **A**: Look at number 8 on page 97. Complete the text by asking **B** questions.
Student **B**: Look at number 8 on page 100. Complete the text by asking **A** questions.
Do not look at each other's texts until you have finished.

2

Meridian Trail

Meridian Trail: a game for three–five players.

You need:
* a dice
* the Trail board on page 102–103
* a small piece of paper with your name on it to use as a 'counter'

How to play
1. Throw the dice. The player with the top score starts the game.
2. The player throws the dice. If, for example, the dice shows 4, he goes forward four squares.
3. If a player lands on, for example, a *GO TO 6* square, he goes forward to square number 6. If he lands on a *GO BACK TO 3* square, he goes back to square number 3.
4. *RISK:* When a player lands on a *RISK* square, all the players must look at the *RISK* questions on page 75. For unit 18, the player must choose the number between 11–20 on the *RISK* square and answer the question. If the other players say 'correct', he goes forward one square. If they say 'wrong', he goes back one square. If in doubt, ask the teacher.
5. The winner is the first player at number 30.

Listening

The Air Taxi Mystery: a radio drama in 9 parts

The story so far... *Detective Inspector Wade knows who the murderer is. She has asked everyone to the offices of the Cutter Air Taxi Service. They are waiting for the murderer to arrive.*

Part 9: The Solution

1

Read the three possible solutions and then listen to the cassette. Which solution is correct?

a Glenda killed Rose because Rose knew about Robert Cutter's murder. Glenda killed Robert and she was going to kill Sarah. Glenda wanted the Cutter Air Taxi Service for her husband, Brian.

b Rose committed suicide because she knew about Robert Cutter's murder by Sarah, his wife. Rose was in love with Robert and couldn't live without him. Sarah killed Robert because she wanted the company.

c Barry killed Rose because Rose didn't want to marry him. He put poison in her coffee. Robert's death was an accident. Robert had a heart attack and his plane flew out to sea.

2

1. Have a press conference and interview Inspector Wade and Sergeant Pride about:

   a who killed Rose Melville and Robert Cutter.
   b why they were killed.
   c how they were killed.

2. Use the information from the press conference to write a newspaper report about the deaths of Rose Melville and Robert Cutter.

A

1

Everyone who is interested in motor racing knows Ricardo Lopes, the racing driver. He was married from 1983–1985 but his wife died. He has one child, a boy.

Ricardo won the Monza Grand Prix in 1984, and he broke the record for that event. He nearly died in 1985. His car skidded and hit a crowd barrier. Luckily no one was seriously injured.

In his free time Ricardo likes to hunt and shoot. Every summer he goes to Spain and watches bull fighting, his favourite sport.

2

Mr Smith	He wanted to get to a meeting on time yesterday, but he didn't.	**Reason?** There was too much traffic.
Mrs Smith	She has wanted to write to her mother all week, but she hasn't.	
Jane Smith	She works in a factory, but she isn't working today.	She is on holiday.
Carol Smith	She wanted to buy a new dress last Saturday, but she didn't.	
John and Tom Smith	They haven't done any homework this week.	Their usual teacher is ill.
Granny Smith	She normally reads in the afternoon, but she isn't reading now.	

3

4

5

CAR MAGAZINE ROAD TEST

	Arena	Trio	Safari
Price			
Size	3.10m × 2.00m	3.60m × 2.45m	3.50m × 2.20m
Top speed	125 kph	200 kph	180 kph
Petrol consumption			
Comfort	**	***	*
Reliability	*	**	***
Quietness			
Stability	**	***	*
Design	**	***	*

kph = kilometres per hour   L/100 km = litres per 100 kilometres

A

6

7

The *Chesholt Culture Club* is a club for men and women over 30 who live in Chesholt. Members of the club meet every Thursday evening and listen to records of classical music. Then they have a 'social half hour'. The club's president is Sir John Pickett and the secretary is Lady Windermere Trout. The *Chesholt Culture Club* has a number of rules. They are:

* Members must not consume any alcohol at club evenings.
* Members must not bring any non-members to the club evenings without permission.
* Members must not fall asleep at club evenings.
* Members must bring one record to each meeting.
* Members must always arrive on time.
* Members must pay £5.00 every month.

8

Tim Stern is a .... and he's 35 years old. He's been married for ten years and he has .... children.

A film cameraman has a busy life. For example, on Wednesday at 10 p.m. he'll be ...., and on Thursday evening he'll probably be filming a first division football match.

Tim hopes he'll be a producer in a few years, but he thinks he'll probably ....

In their spare time Tim and his family like to travel. In past years they've been to .... (1976), Zimbabwe (1980) and Argentina (...............). In two weeks' time Tim and his wife are going to .... The children aren't going with them; they're staying at home with their grandparents.

B

1

Bruno Marini is not married and he has no children. Sailing takes up most of his life.

Bruno won the solo Transatlantic race in 1979, 1982 and 1985, but he didn't break the 1975 American record. He has never been in any danger at sea. In his free time Bruno paints and reads novels. Every summer he goes to Florence to visit the museums.

2

Mr Smith	He wanted to get to a meeting on time yesterday, but he didn't.	**Reason?**
Mrs Smith	She has wanted to write to her mother all week, but she hasn't.	She has been very busy.
Jane Smith	She works in a factory, but she isn't working today.	
Carol Smith	She wanted to buy a new dress last Saturday, but she didn't.	She didn't have enough money.
John and Tom Smith	They haven't done any homework this week.	
Granny Smith	She normally reads in the afternoon, but she isn't reading now.	She is watching the racing on TV.

3

B

4

5

CAR MAGAZINE ROAD TEST			
	Arena	Trio	Safari
Price	£10,000	£25,000	£19,000
Size			
Top speed	125 kph	200 kph	180 kph
Petrol consumption	6 L/100 km	8 L/100 km	7 L/100 km
Comfort			
Reliability	*	**	***
Quietness	**	*	***
Stability			
Design	**	***	*

kph = kilometres per hour

L/100 km = litres per 100 kilometres

B

6

7

The *Naseby Culture Club* is a club for women of any age who live in Naseby. Members of the club meet every Thursday morning and paint pictures of birds and flowers. Then they have a 'social half hour'. The club's president is Mary Daffy and the secretary is Maude Salmon.
The *Naseby Culture Club* has a number of rules. They are:

* Members must not consume any alcohol at club mornings.
* Members must not bring any non-members to the club meetings without permission.
* Members must not copy each others' work.
* Members must bring their own paints and materials.
* Members must clean up the hall after each morning.
* Members must pay £1.50 every Thursday.

8

Tim Stern is a film cameraman and he's .... years old. He's been married for .... years and he has three children.

A film cameraman has a busy life. For example, on Wednesday at 10 p.m. he'll be filming a boxing match, and on Thursday evening he'll probably be

....

Tim hopes he'll be a .... in a few years, but he thinks he'll probably still be a cameraman.

In their spare time Tim and his family like to travel. In past years they've been to Australia (1976), Zimbabwe (...............) and .... (1984). In two weeks' time Tim and his wife are going to Japan. The children aren't going with them; they're staying at home with their

....

9

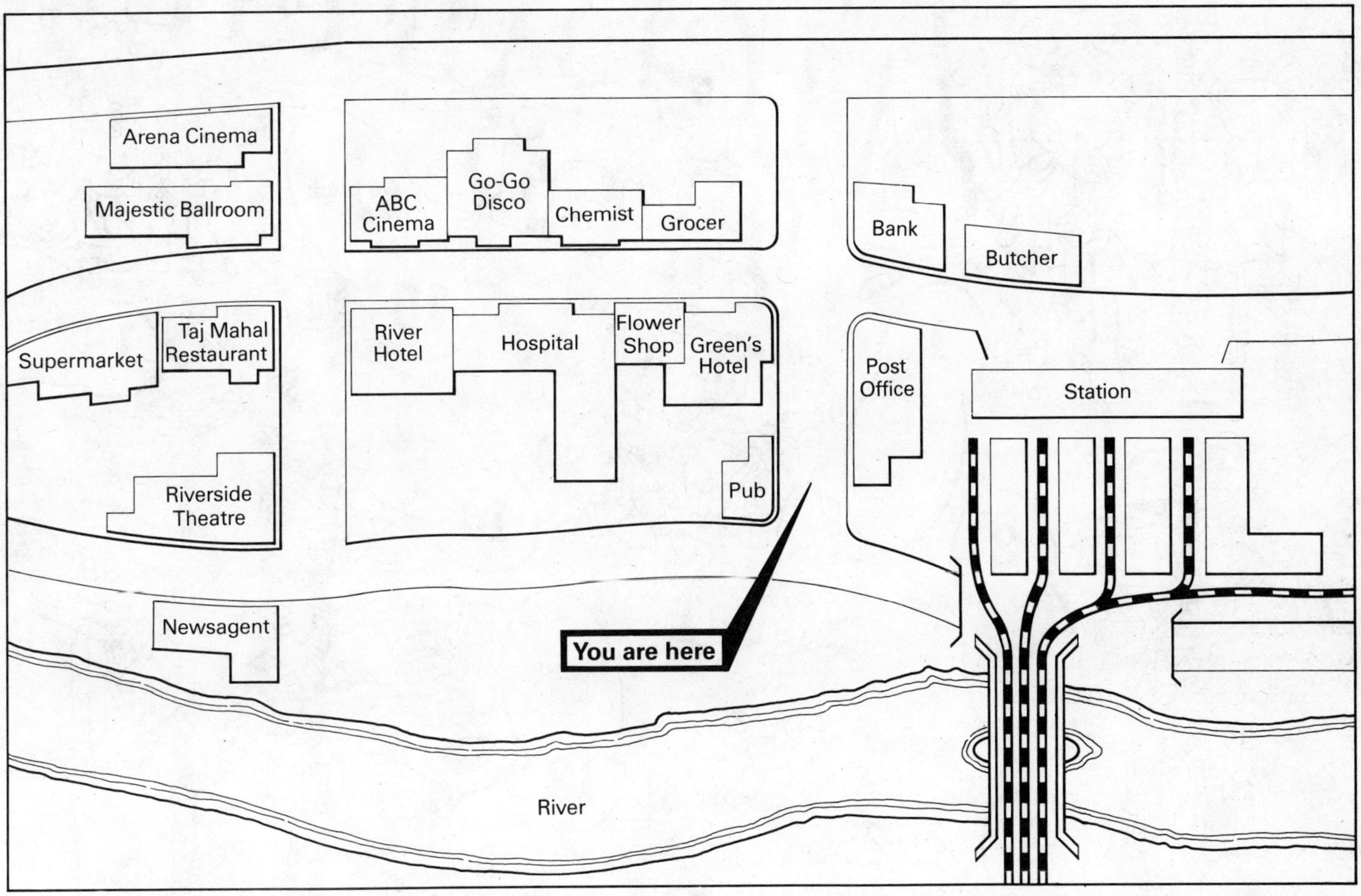

Arena Cinema
Majestic Ballroom
ABC Cinema
Go-Go Disco
Chemist
Grocer
Bank
Butcher
Supermarket
Taj Mahal Restaurant
River Hotel
Hospital
Flower Shop
Green's Hotel
Post Office
Station
Pub
Riverside Theatre
Newsagent
You are here
River

Meridian Trail
1
2 RISK 1/11
3
4 Go to 6
5 RISK 2/12
6 RISK 3/13
7 Go back to 3
8
9
10 Go to 12
11 RISK 4/14
12 Go to 16
13 RISK 5/15
14
15 Go back to 8
16 RISK 6/16
27
28
29 RISK 10/20
30

Meridian Trail: Risks 1–10

1 Complete the sequence:
tall/taller/tallest; big/bigger/biggest; good/........../..........

2 Which is correct? He isn't as **a** *bigger* **b** *biggest* **c** *big* as his brother.

3 Complete this sentence:
Books are .... expensive than records.

4 Complete the sequence:
wear/wore/worn; work/worked/worked;
kick/........../..........; go/........../..........

5 Give the correct form of the verb in brackets:
I (never see) .... the film 'A Passage to India'.

6 Make a sentence with *just*.

7 Complete this sentence with one word only:
I haven't got .... money.

8 Complete the following sequence:
kind/unkind; expensive/inexpensive; possible/..........

9 Make a question with *most expensive*.

10 Which is correct? He **a** *has* **b** *was* just been made President.

Meridian Trail: Risks 11–20

11 Complete this sentence with one word only:
You weren't at home last night, ... you?

12 Give the correct form of the verb in brackets:
Next week I (buy) a new car.

13 Make a question with *been*.

14 Which is correct? I haven't seen him **a** *since* **b** *for* two years.

15 Complete the sequence:
see/saw/seen; wear/wore/worn; speak/........../..........

16 Give the correct forms of the verbs in brackets:
If you (go) out now, you (get) .... wet.

17 Make a sentence with *as soon as*.

18 Which is correct? If I **a** *win* **b** *will win* a lot of money, I'll buy a car.

19 Make a question with *while*.

20 Which is correct? As soon as he **a** *will arrive* **b** *has arrived* he'll phone his wife.

10

5

CAR MAGAZINE ROAD TEST			
	Arena	Trio	Safari
Price	£10,000	£25,000	£19,000
Size	3.10m × 2.00m	3.60m × 2.45m	3.50m × 2.20m
Top speed			
Petrol consumption	6 L/100 km	8 L/100 km	7 L/100 km
Comfort	**	***	*
Reliability			
Quietness	**	*	***
Stability	**	***	*
Design			

kph = kilometres per hour L/100 km = litres per 100 kilometres

6

Tapescript

Unit 1

ANNOUNCER: Murder at Walton Hall.

ANNOUNCER: Part 1. Friday Evening.
SALLY: Thank you . . . good night.
ANNE: Good evening, Miss Walton.
SALLY: Good evening, Anne. It's very late. Why aren't you in bed?
ANNE: I'm going in a minute, Miss Walton, but I have to take your mother her hot milk.
SALLY: Yes, of course. Er. . . where's my father?
ANNE: In the sitting room.
SALLY: How is he?
ANNE: How is he? He's not feeling very well, actually.
SALLY: I'd better go and see him, then. Good night, Anne.
ANNE: Good night, Miss Walton.
MR WALTON: Oh. . . Hello, love.
SALLY: Hello, Daddy. . . How are you?
MR WALTON: I'm not feeling very well, actually. But I'll be all right in the morning. What about you? Did you like the show?
SALLY: Oh yes! I thought it was fantastic. All the actors and actresses were on roller skates and they were. . .
MR WALTON: Who did you go with?
SALLY: Er. . . with Bruce.
MR WALTON: Ah. . . Bruce.
SALLY: Are you angry with me?
MR WALTON: Look, Sally, you're an adult now. You're nearly 21 years old!
SALLY: But what about Mummy?
MR WALTON: Your mother doesn't like Bruce, and frankly, I can't say. . .
ANNE: Help! Help! Somebody please help!
SALLY: Anne! What's the matter? Why are you shouting like that?
ANNE: It's your mother, Miss Walton. She's dead!

Unit 2

ANNOUNCER: Murder at Walton Hall.

ANNOUNCER: Part 2. The Next Morning.
PRIDE: Good morning. Is Mr Walton in, please? We're police officers and we'd like to speak to him.
ANNE: Oh, you must be Inspector Wade.
WADE: No, he isn't. I'm Inspector Wade.
ANNE: Oh, I'm sorry, I thought. . .
WADE: Yes, everybody does. Now then, can we speak to Mr Walton?
ANNE: Well, er. . . Inspector, I'm afraid he's gone out.
WADE: Oh? Do you know where he is?
ANNE: No, I don't. He left the house at 6 o'clock in the morning. He's never gone out that early before.
WADE: Yes, I see. Is Miss Walton at home?
ANNE: Yes, she's in the gym with Mr Carter. Would you like to talk to her?
WADE: Yes, I think that would be a good idea. Come along, Sergeant.
ANNE: Inspector Wade and Sergeant Pride are here, Miss Walton.
SALLY: Oh! Which is which?
PRIDE: I'm Sergeant Pride.
WADE: And I'm Inspector Wade.
SALLY: Have you found the killer, Inspector?
WADE: Not yet, Miss Walton. But we do know what killed her.
SALLY: What was that?
WADE: Your mother was poisoned, Miss Walton. We think that the poison was in her food at dinner.
BRUCE: Well then, we know who the murderer is!
PRIDE: And who are you sir?
SALLY: This is Bruce Carter, Sergeant. He's my boyfriend.
WADE: We're pleased to meet you, Mr Carter. So we know who the murderer is, do we?
BRUCE: Yes, of course. It was Anne, of course! She prepares Mr and Mrs Walton's food every evening. Ask her about the murder.
SALLY: Well, Anne? Are you the murderer? Did you poison my mother?
ANNE: No, I did not. It wasn't me. I didn't kill Mrs Walton. You know I didn't.

Unit 3

ANNOUNCER: Murder at Walton Hall.

ANNOUNCER: Part 3. A Telephone Call.
STAN: 377023. Hello.
ANNE: Hello, Stan. It's me. Anne.
STAN: Anne?
ANNE: Yes, Stan, it's me!
STAN: Well. . . hello.
ANNE: Can I come and see you?
STAN: What, now?
ANNE: Yes, now. I've got to talk to you.
STAN: But you've never been to my house before.
ANNE: I know. But I've got to talk to you.
STAN: What about?
ANNE: I can't talk on the phone. Can I come over? Please!
STAN: All right. All right. You'd better come.
ANNE: Oh thanks, Stan. How do I get to your house?
STAN: Where are you now?
ANNE: At a phone booth next to the bridge — there's a church opposite.
STAN: OK. Right, now listen. Go across the bridge and keep going until you reach the crossroads. Take the first turning on your right and cross the second bridge. OK so far?
ANNE: Yes. Yes, I think so.
STAN: So you're over the second bridge. Go down the second turning on your left until you get to River Close. Then turn right and go along River Close for about 50 metres and it's on your right, opposite the cinema.
ANNE: So it's first on the right. . . over the bridge. . . second right.
STAN: No, no, no. First right, second left. . . *left.* Hello? Anne? Can you hear me, Anne? Are you there?

Unit 4

ANNOUNCER: Murder at Walton Hall.

ANNOUNCER: Part 4. Coffee.
WADE: The heater in this car isn't working. I'm freezing.
PRIDE: Me too, Inspector. Shall we stop and have a coffee?
WADE: Yes, John. That's a good idea.
PRIDE: Well, Inspector, do you know who poisoned Mrs Walton?
WADE: Not yet, not yet, John. There are too many questions and not enough answers.
PRIDE: What about the husband, Mr Walton?
WADE: Yes, I'm interested in Mr Walton. He's disappeared — even Sally Walton doesn't know where he is.
PRIDE: What about Anne Clark?
WADE: The maid, you mean?
PRIDE: Yes.
WADE: Well, it's possible, but I can't think of a reason.
PRIDE: And the gardener, Stan?
WADE: That's possible. Actually I'm more interested in Mr Bruce Carter.
PRIDE: Sally's boyfriend.
WADE: Yes. I think I've seen him before.
PRIDE: But he was with Sally at the theatre when Mrs Walton was poisoned.
WADE: Yes, I know. But I'm sure I know him.
PRIDE: What are we going to do now, Inspector?
WADE: We're going to see Vanessa Walton.
PRIDE: *Vanessa* Walton? Who's she?
WADE: Sally's big sister.
PRIDE: I didn't know that Sally had a sister.
WADE: Well, she does. She lives in London — she left home three years ago I understand. Finish your coffee and we'll go.

WADE: You'd better call up control, John.
PRIDE: Right, Inspector. Calling control. This is car 27. Any messages? Over.
RADIO: Hello, car 27. Yes. We've got another murder for you. A young lady called Anne Clark. She was killed at the phone booth on Alexander Bridge. Over.
WADE: OK, John. Forget about Vanessa Walton. Get me to that bridge. Quickly!

Unit 5

ANNOUNCER: Murder at Walton Hall.

ANNOUNCER: Part 5. Vanessa.

WADE: Why was Anne killed? What did she know, I wonder?

PRIDE: The name of the killer?

WADE: Yes, I think so. But who was it? And was Anne murdered by Mrs Walton's killer? Or was it somebody else?

PRIDE: This is Station Road, Inspector. Vanessa Walton lives at number 27.

WADE: This isn't a very nice area.

PRIDE: No, it isn't. Why is Vanessa Walton living here?

WADE: That's a good question. The Waltons are very rich.

PRIDE: Here we are, Inspector.

VANESSA: Yes?

WADE: Miss Vanessa Walton?

VANESSA: Yes.

WADE: We're police officers. We want to talk to you.

VANESSA: I can't tell you anything. I don't want to talk to you. Goodbye.

PRIDE: Open the door, Miss Walton. Let us in.

WADE: That's better. Now then, Miss Walton, let's have a little talk.

VANESSA: I'm not going to tell you anything.

WADE: Why do you live in this horrible place?

VANESSA: What's wrong with it?

WADE: Nothing. But why don't you live in a bigger, cleaner house? You're not poor. Your family's got lots of money.

VANESSA: I've spent my money. I haven't got any left.

PRIDE: What did you spend it on, Miss Walton? Clothes? Food? Holidays?

WADE: Or was it drugs?

VANESSA: I don't know what you're talking about. I'm not going to. . .

WADE: You're a drug addict, aren't you? What is it? Heroin? Cocaine?

VANESSA: Heroin, if you want to know.

PRIDE: When did you last go home, Miss Walton?

VANESSA: Three weeks ago. I haven't been home for three weeks. . . What are you looking at me like that for? I didn't kill my mother.

Unit 6

ANNOUNCER: Murder at Walton Hall.

ANNOUNCER: Part 6. Stan the Gardener.

STAN: Yes?

PRIDE: Mr Williams? Stan Williams?

STAN: Yes?

PRIDE: My name's Sergeant Pride. Can I have a word with you?

STAN: It's about the murders, is it?

PRIDE: Yes.

STAN: You'd better come in. I'll just switch off the television.

PRIDE: Now, Mr Williams, you work as a gardener at Walton Hall?

STAN: Yes.

PRIDE: And how long have you worked there?

STAN: For five years.

PRIDE: What about Anne?

STAN: She's been here. . . she came to Walton Hall six months ago.

PRIDE: Mr Williams, has Anne been worried recently?

STAN: Worried?

PRIDE: Was Anne nervous? Unhappy?

STAN: Yes, yes, she was.

PRIDE: Why?

STAN: It was the day before Mrs Walton's death. Thursday, it was. Anne was in the kitchen doing the washing up. She heard two people talking in the garden outside the kitchen window.

PRIDE: Who were they, Stan?

STAN: One of them was Miss Walton.

PRIDE: Sally Walton?

STAN: No, sir. Her sister, Vanessa.

PRIDE: That is interesting! Who was the other person?

STAN: Mr Burton, the local chemist.

PRIDE: And Anne told you about this?

STAN: Yes. She was very worried.

PRIDE: Why?

STAN: Well, they were having an argument. Miss Vanessa was very angry, Anne said.

PRIDE: That's very interesting information, Mr Williams. Is that all you can tell me?

STAN: No, Sergeant. Anne rang me up on Saturday night. She wanted to come and talk to me. She was very frightened. And then. . .

PRIDE: Yes, Mr Williams?

STAN: I heard her murder. . .

WADE: How did you get on with Mr Williams, John?

PRIDE: Well, Inspector, I've learnt something very interesting about Vanessa!

WADE: And I've learnt something interesting about Mr Bruce Carter. Did you know that he was in prison for three years?

PRIDE: What for?

WADE: He sold drugs — especially heroin.

Unit 7

ANNOUNCER: Murder at Walton Hall.

ANNOUNCER: Part 7. At The Chemist's.
ASSISTANT: Good morning. Can I help you?
PRIDE: Er. . . yes, please. We'd like to speak to Mr Burton, if that's possible.
ASSISTANT: If you just wait a minute, I'll go and get him.
PRIDE: Thank you.
WADE: What have you got there, Sergeant?
PRIDE: I don't know. It says 'moisturizing cream'.
WADE: Ugh. . . it looks horrible!
PRIDE: Yes. But it smells OK.
BURTON: Can I help you?
WADE: Yes, Mr Burton, I think you can.
BURTON: I'm sorry?
WADE: We're police officers, Mr Burton. I'm Inspector Wade and this is Sergeant Pride.
BURTON: Oh! Well why do you want to see me?
WADE: I want to know the answers to two questions, Mr Burton. Why did you go to Walton Hall last Thursday, and what did you say to Miss Vanessa Walton?
BURTON: I. . . er. . .
PRIDE: We want answers, Mr Burton. We'll wait if we have to.
BURTON: All right. I went to Walton Hall to be a witness.
WADE: A witness?
BURTON: Yes. To David Walton's will.
PRIDE: Didn't he have a will already?
BURTON: Oh, yes. But he wanted to change it.
WADE: Ah. . . So Mr Walton made a new will.
BURTON: Yes.
WADE: What was in this new will, Mr Burton?
BURTON: I. . . er. . . I can't remember.
WADE: Oh dear! Well, what about the second question? Tell us about Vanessa.
BURTON: Vanessa?
PRIDE: Yes, Mr Burton. Why were you two arguing outside the kitchen window at Walton Hall last Thursday?
BURTON: Arguing?
WADE: Come on, Mr Burton. Let's have some answers. Two people have been killed already.
BURTON: But I can't tell you about Vanessa. I. . . er. . . I can't remember.
WADE: Did she ask you for drugs? You're a chemist. Did she ask you for more heroin?
BURTON: I don't know! I can't remember.
WADE: Maybe you'll remember down at the police station. Bring him along, Sergeant.
PRIDE: Come along, sir.
BURTON: Take your hands off me! Let me go!
WALTON: Stop that. Leave Mr Burton alone. I can tell you everything.
WADE: And who are you?
WALTON: My name's Walton. David Walton.
WADE: Ah, Mr Walton! Pleased to meet you.

Unit 8

ANNOUNCER: Murder at Walton Hall.

ANNOUNCER: Part 8. Mr Walton's Story.
WALTON: How long are you going to keep me here, Inspector?
WADE: Not long, Mr Walton. I just want some answers to some questions.
WALTON: Well, how can I help you?
WADE: Mr Walton, on the evening of your wife's murder, what did she eat for supper?
WALTON: Who? My wife?
WADE: Yes.
WALTON: The usual things, I think.
PRIDE: And what about you, Mr Walton? What did you have?
WALTON: I was feeling ill. I only had a bowl of soup.
WADE: And what about your wife?
WALTON: She had. . . er. . . toast and. . .
PRIDE: And what, Mr Walton?
WALTON: And margarine.
WADE: Wait a minute, Mr Walton. What's so strange about that? Doesn't she usually eat margarine?
WALTON: No. She always eats butter. I'm the one who likes margarine. I have a heart condition, you see, and margarine isn't as fattening as butter. It hasn't got as much cholesterol as butter — and anyway it's cheaper, so if you have a heart cond. . .
WADE: Thank you for the lecture, Mr Walton. But why did your wife have margarine that evening?
WALTON: Well, Anne Clark had forgotten to buy butter, so my wife didn't have any alternative!
WADE: So that was it.
WALTON: Do you know who the murderer is, Inspector?
WADE: Oh, yes. I know who, but I don't know why. You're going to tell me.
WALTON: But I. . .
PRIDE: Why did you disappear from Walton Hall? Where have you been for the last few days?
WALTON: I've been here with Mr Burton.
PRIDE: Why, Mr Walton? Why hide with Mr Burton?
WALTON: My wife's death! I was very upset.
PRIDE: You know who the murderer is, don't you, Mr Walton?
WALTON: I. . . no. . . no, I don't.
WADE: Let's talk about your will, Mr Walton.
WALTON: My will?
WADE: Yes, the new will you made the day before the murder.
WALTON: I'm going to have to tell you everything, aren't I?
WADE: Yes, Mr Walton. That is the general idea.
WALTON: All right. It can't make the situation worse. Look, to understand this you have to know about Vanessa and her problems.
WADE: Come on, John. Let's go and get Mrs Walton's killer.

Unit 9

ANNOUNCER: Murder at Walton Hall.

ANNOUNCER: Part 9. The Arrest.

SALLY: Oh, good evening, Inspector.

WADE: Hello, Miss Walton. Can we come in?

SALLY: Yes, of course.

WADE: Ah, Mr Carter, good evening. I am pleased to see you here.

CARTER: Why, Inspector? And why have you come here this evening?

WADE: Mr Carter, which is more expensive, heroin or cocaine?

CARTER: Well it depends on the quality, but. . .

PRIDE: You're quite an expert, aren't you Mr Carter?

SALLY: Leave my boyfriend alone, Sergeant Pride.

PRIDE: In a minute, Miss Walton. When did you first meet Vanessa, Mr Carter?

CARTER: About two years ago.

WADE: And you sold her drugs. You gave her heroin, didn't you?

CARTER: I. . . er. . .

WADE: That's how you make your money, isn't it, Mr Carter? You sell drugs to people like Vanessa. You get them hooked and ruin their lives for ever.

CARTER: I want to see a lawyer.

WADE: Don't worry, Mr Carter, you will. Take him away, Constable. Get him out of here.

CARTER: I protest. I'm not going to. . .

SALLY: What are you going to do with him?

WADE: You really love him don't you?

SALLY: Yes. . . yes, I do.

WADE: And you would do anything for him, wouldn't you?

SALLY: Yes.

PRIDE: Like murder, Miss Walton?

SALLY: What are you talking about?

WADE: Miss Walton, I arrest you for the murder of your mother, Mrs Irene Walton, and the maid, Anne Clark.

SALLY: But that's ridiculous! I didn't want to kill Mummy.

WADE: No, Miss Walton. You wanted to kill your father.

SALLY: Nonsense! You're talking nonsense! Give me one reason why I would want to kill my own father.

PRIDE: The oldest reason in the world, Miss Walton, money.

WADE: Yes, it was because of your father's will, wasn't it?

SALLY: I don't know what you're talking about.

WADE: Oh yes you do. Your father knew about your sister Vanessa and your boyfriend Bruce Carter. So he made a new will. You don't get any money, do you, if you marry Bruce Carter?

SALLY: Well no, but I. . .

PRIDE: As Mrs Bruce Carter you lose everything, don't you? All the money goes to Vanessa.

WADE: So you tried to kill your father, collect the money from his will, and then marry Bruce Carter. And then you had to kill Anne Clark because she knew about your mother's murder.

SALLY: But I love him. I love Bruce.

WADE: Yes, Miss Walton, I'm sure you do. Take her away, Sergeant.

PRIDE: Well, Sally Walton's going to be in prison for a long time.

WADE: Yes, but what about Bruce Carter? When is he going to start selling drugs again? He's much more dangerous than all the Sally Waltons in the world.

PRIDE: Yes. . . Shall we go and have something to eat at that new sandwich bar?

WADE: Yes, why not? I'm going to have an enormous cheese and tomato sandwich, made with butter.

PRIDE: Butter, Inspector?

WADE: Yes, butter. I don't think I want to eat margarine ever again!

Unit 10

ANNOUNCER: The Air Taxi Mystery.

ANNOUNCER: Part 1. The Crash.
PILOT: Wadebridge control — Bravo Delta. I have an emergency.
CONTROLLER: Please state your problem, Bravo Delta.
PILOT: My engine is stopping — I think there's a problem with the fuel pipe.
CONTROLLER: What is your position?
PILOT: I'm not sure. I'm about twenty miles east of Padstow, I think.
CONTROLLER: Can you try and land?
PILOT: Negative. There's too much cloud. Oh no! The engine's cut out. . . and I can't. . . there's something wrong with the rudder. Oh no. . . this is. . . I can't. . .
CONTROLLER: Come in, Bravo Delta. Bravo Delta, are you receiving me? Oh, for heaven's sake! Get me the North Cornwall Police. Quickly!

....

WADE: Oh, Tony, that was the best supper I've ever eaten.
TONY: I'm glad you liked it, Sheila.
WADE: Oh, I did. You're the most fantastic cook!
TONY: No, I'm not! I can only cook moussaka and spaghetti bolognese!
WADE: Oh, Tony, I love coming here.
TONY: Yes, so do I. I'd like to come more often.
WADE: I can't. You know that, Tony. It's not easy being a policewoman, you know.
TONY: It's not easy being a policewoman's husband, either!
WADE: And Cornwall is a very long way from London.
TONY: Yes, but we bought this cottage as a weekend holiday home, and we never come here because you're always too busy, and. . .
WADE: What on earth's that? It's coming this way. Tony, watch out!

Unit 11

ANNOUNCER: The Air Taxi Mystery.

ANNOUNCER: Part 2. The Constable's Story.
WADE: Well, that's over with. Shall I make a cup of tea, Tony?
TONY: No, thanks. But I'll make some coffee in a minute, if you want.
WADE: Yes. Yes, that's a good idea.
TONY: What a night!
WADE: Yes, but at least the plane missed the house.
TONY: Only just!
WADE: Look, Tony, it nearly killed us, but it didn't. We're still here. What about that coffee?
TONY: It did kill the pilot though, didn't it? Do they know who he was?
WADE: I don't think so, no. Everything was very badly burnt.
POLICEMAN: I just came to say good night, Inspector Wade — or rather good morning, now.
WADE: Oh, are you off?
POLICEMAN: Yes, ma'am. We've done everything we can for the moment.
WADE: How long have you been a policeman, Constable?
POLICEMAN: Nearly ten months now.
WADE: Have you ever had to deal with an aeroplane accident before?
POLICEMAN: No, ma'am. This is my first.
WADE: It's not pretty, is it?
POLICEMAN: No, it isn't. I feel sorry for the pilot.
WADE: Yes.
POLICEMAN: I wonder why she crashed.
TONY: The kettle's boiled. I'm making the coffee.
WADE: OK. I'm coming in a second.
POLICEMAN: Oh well, I'll say goodnight, ma'am.
WADE: Wait a minute, Constable. Did you say 'she'?
POLICEMAN: Yes, Inspector. The pilot was female and we think — my Superintendent thinks — she opened the door before she crashed.
WADE: Oh well, for once it's not my case. I'm on holiday.
POLICEMAN: And I hope you enjoy it, Inspector Wade. Goodbye.
WADE: Goodbye, Constable. Why did she open the door, I wonder? It doesn't make sense. No, I don't understand it. Unless. . .

Unit 12

ANNOUNCER: The Air Taxi Mystery.

ANNOUNCER: Part 3. The Chief Investigator.
PRIDE: Did you enjoy your weekend, Inspector?
WADE: No, John, I did not. I was nearly killed by a Cessna Citation!
PRIDE: By what?
WADE: A Cessna Citation. It's a type of aeroplane, Sergeant.
PRIDE: Ah! What happened?
WADE: It was about quarter past ten in the evening. We were sitting in the dining room of our house after a delicious supper. We were talking, when suddenly we heard this screaming engine and a plane smashed into the field next to the house.
PRIDE: But you weren't hurt, Inspector?
WADE: No, we were all right. Of course the pilot was killed — a woman, I understand. But there are one or two things about the crash that puzzle me.
RADIO: Calling Inspector Wade. Calling Detective Inspector Wade.
WADE: Wade here, over.
RADIO: Oh, hello, Sheila. George here. Could you go to the Aviation Accident Board in Barclay Street and report to the Chief Investigator? Over.
WADE: Yes, of course, but why? Over.
RADIO: He wants to talk to you about that aeroplane crash.
WADE: All right. We're on our way!
MASON: Can I help you?
PRIDE: Yes, please. We want to speak to the Chief Investigator. We're from the police.
MASON: Ah yes, Inspector Wade, isn't it?
PRIDE: Oh, no. I'm Sergeant Pride.
MASON: Well, where's Inspector Wade?
WADE: I'm Inspector Wade.
MASON: You are? I didn't realize the police. . .
WADE: Are you the Chief Investigator?
MASON: Yes, I am. My name's Mason. Look, I *am* sorry. It's just that, well, I didn't expect. . .
WADE: You didn't expect an Inspector to be a woman! Times are changing, Mr Mason.
MASON: Yes, yes of course.
WADE: Now then, how can I help you?
MASON: Erm. . . you saw the aeroplane crash, didn't you?
WADE: Not exactly, no. But I heard it.
MASON: Oh. But I'd like you to hear this anyway — to see if you can help us at all.
PRIDE: What are we going to hear?
MASON: A recording of the pilot's last message. Here goes.
PILOT: My engine is stopping — I think there's a problem with the fuel pipe.
CONTROLLER: What is your position?
PILOT: I'm not sure. I'm about twenty miles east of Padstow, I think.
CONTROLLER: Can you try and land?
PILOT: Negative. There's too much cloud. Oh no! The engine's cut out. . . and I can't. . . there's something wrong with the rudder. Oh no. . . this is. . . I can't. . .
MASON: That's all there is.
WADE: What time was this?
MASON: We lost contact at. . . er. . . exactly. . . 2203 hours — three minutes past ten.
WADE: That's very strange.
MASON: Why?
WADE: You lost contact at three minutes past ten, but the plane didn't crash until twenty past. I heard it. What happened in those seventeen minutes?

Unit 13

ANNOUNCER: The Air Taxi Mystery.

ANNOUNCER: Part 4. The Cutter Air Taxi Service.
BRIAN: Morning!
SARAH: Good morning.
BRIAN: It's a bad morning for you, isn't it?
SARAH: Well, yes. Yes, it is. First Robert, now Rose.
BRIAN: There's no connection. Rose had engine failure. She was flying along quite happily and then her engine cut out.
SARAH: But why? The plane was given a complete service the day before.
BRIAN: I know. I don't understand it, either.
SARAH: Where's Glenda?
BRIAN: Oh, yes. She asked me to give you a message. She's too upset to come in today.
SARAH: Well so am I, but I'm here. Why doesn't she. . .
BRIAN: Careful Sarah! You *are* my sister, but that doesn't mean you can be rude about my wife!
SARAH: Oh, I'm sorry Brian. It's just that. . . Oh. Good morning. Can I help you?
WADE: I hope so. We're looking for the Cutter Air Taxi Service.
SARAH: Well, you've come to the right place.
WADE: Good. We want to speak to the owner of the company. Is that you by any chance?
SARAH: Yes. I'm Sarah Cutter. . .
WADE: Well, I'm Detective Inspector Wade and this is Sergeant Pride.
BRIAN: Police! What are you doing here?
WADE: We're making enquiries into the death of Rose Melville.
SARAH: But the plane crash was an accident, wasn't it?
PRIDE: We're just making some enquiries, Mrs Cutter.
SARAH: What do you want to know?
WADE: Could you tell us who works in the company, Mrs Cutter?
SARAH: Of course. I own Cutter Air Taxis and my brother Brian is the business manager.
PRIDE: That's you, sir, is it?
BRIAN: That's right.
SARAH: Brian's wife, Glenda, is one of our pilots.
WADE: Do you fly, too, Mrs Cutter?
SARAH: Yes, but I haven't flown much recently. Rose did all my flying.
WADE: Yes, I see. Is there anyone else?
SARAH: Yes, there's Barry, our mechanic.
PRIDE: Is that everyone?
SARAH: Yes.
WADE: This isn't the first time, is it? This is the second death for Cutter Air, isn't it?
SARAH: Yes. My husband, Robert, was killed in a crash six months ago.
PRIDE: Was that an accident too, Mrs Cutter?

Unit 14

ANNOUNCER: The Air Taxi Mystery.

ANNOUNCER: Part 5. Robert Cutter's Story.
SECRETARY: Good morning, can I help you?
WADE: Yes, please. I'd like to speak to the Chief Investigator.
SECRETARY: Can I have your name, please?
WADE: Yes, certainly. I'm Detective Inspector Wade and this is Sergeant Pride.
SECRETARY: Well, if you wait here, I'll go and see if he's free.
PRIDE: I hope Mr Mason will see us.
WADE: Of course he will.
PRIDE: He was rather embarrassed when we were here before.
WADE: Oh, I'm sure he won't remember that.
SECRETARY: Mr Mason will see you now. Please come this way.
MASON: Come in. Ah yes, Detective Inspector Wade. I remember our last meeting. Come in, Sergeant.
PRIDE: Thank you, Mr Mason.
MASON: How are you getting on with the enquiry, Inspector?
WADE: Not too badly. But there are a lot of things I don't understand.
MASON: Can I help?
WADE: I hope so. What can you remember about Robert Cutter's death?
MASON: That was about six months ago, wasn't it?
WADE: Yes, that's right.
MASON: It was a strange case. Cutter was an experienced pilot — I don't really understand it at all.
WADE: What happened exactly?
MASON: Well, he took off one morning and flew south towards Cornwall. He was going to deliver an old clock to an American living there. But for some reason he turned west and flew out over the sea.
PRIDE: What happened?
MASON: He just kept flying on and on — I imagine he ran out of fuel in the end.
WADE: Did they find his body?
MASON: No.
WADE: Well how do you know what happened to him?
MASON: A passing ship found some wreckage — part of a door — and it came from Cutter's aeroplane.
WADE: Another door. Mmm. That is interesting!
MASON: Inspector?
WADE: Mr Mason, you've been very helpful. Thank you very much. Come on, Sergeant.
MASON: Don't mention it. Anything I can do to help. . .

Unit 15

ANNOUNCER: The Air Taxi Mystery.

ANNOUNCER: Part 6. Barry.
SARAH: How can I help you, Inspector?
WADE: We would like to speak to your mechanic, if that's possible, Mrs Cutter.
SARAH: You mean Barry?
WADE: Yes.
SARAH: He's in that big grey hangar over there. He's working on a red and green Piper Cub.
WADE: Would you go and talk to him, John?
PRIDE: Yes, of course.
WADE: Mrs Cutter, I have got some more questions for you.
SARAH: Must I answer them?
WADE: You don't have to, of course, but I need some information — and I intend to get it.
SARAH: Of course. I was only joking.
WADE: Yes, I'm sure you were. Do you have any relations, Mrs Cutter?
SARAH: Only my brother Brian. My parents died years ago.
WADE: And when your husband died, did you get all his money?
SARAH: Most of it, yes — and I took over the company. Why? Why all these questions?
WADE: I just want to understand the whole story, Mrs Cutter.
PRIDE: Hello!
BARRY: Hello.
PRIDE: Are you Barry?
BARRY: That's right. Who are you?
PRIDE: I'm Sergeant Pride — from the police.
BARRY: Oh. What do you want?
PRIDE: Just some questions about Rose Melville's aircraft. Was it in good condition?
BARRY: It was fine. I gave it a complete service the day before the accident. I'm a good mechanic, Sergeant, so you can't blame me.
PRIDE: I wasn't blaming you. What about Rose?
BARRY: What do you mean?
PRIDE: How did you get on with her?
BARRY: OK. Why do you want to know? I don't know anything!
GLENDA: Barry, Barry darling, we've got to talk, I. . .
BARRY: Glenda! Not now!
GLENDA: Barry, we must. There are. . .
PRIDE: Good afternoon, Mrs Neal.
GLENDA: Who are you?
BARRY: He's a policeman!
PRIDE: Sergeant Pride, madam. Please excuse me. We'll meet again soon. Goodbye.
GLENDA: Er. . . goodbye.

Unit 16

ANNOUNCER: The Air Taxi Mystery.

ANNOUNCER: Part 7. Glenda.
GLENDA: Oh. . . hello.
WADE: Good morning, Mrs Neal. Is your husband in?
GLENDA: No, he's gone to the office.
WADE: Aren't you working today?
GLENDA: Yes, I am later. I'm flying to Scotland this afternoon.
WADE: Oh, why are you going there?
GLENDA: I'm taking some tourists to see Edinburgh.
WADE: It's a beautiful city.
GLENDA: If you say so. Now then, would you like some coffee?
WADE: Yes, that would be nice. What about you, Sergeant?
PRIDE: If you're having some I will too, Inspector.
GLENDA: Well come into the kitchen, then.
WADE: What's this trophy Mrs Neal?
GLENDA: Oh. . . I won that last summer.
WADE: What for? What did you win?
GLENDA: The Southern parachuting championship.
WADE: Oh, so you're an experienced parachutist, then?
GLENDA: Well. . . er. . . yes, I suppose so. Anyway, come and have your coffee.
WADE: How long have you worked for Cutter's?
GLENDA: About a year and a half now. I joined when Robert started the company.
WADE: Do you like your work?
GLENDA: Oh, yes. I love flying.
WADE: What about the other people in the company?
GLENDA: Well, I'm married to one of them!
WADE: Yes, I know. But what about the others? How do you get on with Barry, for example?
GLENDA: Barry? Oh. . . Barry's just a good friend. Umm, he's a good mechanic, and I like him, that's all.
WADE: I see. What about your sister-in-law?
GLENDA: Sarah, you mean?
WADE: Yes.
GLENDA: What about her?
WADE: Was she very upset by her husband's death?
GLENDA: Well, it was strange. She didn't cry when she heard. She always wanted to be the boss of Cutter Air Taxis — even when Robert was alive. But I'm sure she was unhappy about his death. . . I mean, of course she was.
WADE: Of course. Is she a good boss? Do you like working for her?
GLENDA: Yes. Yes, of course.
PRIDE: Well, Inspector, do you think that visit was a success?
WADE: Oh yes, John, I do. We learnt a lot from Mrs Glenda Neal.

Unit 17

ANNOUNCER: The Air Taxi Mystery.

ANNOUNCER: Part 8. Waiting.
PRIDE: Hello, Barry.
BARRY: Oh, it's you again.
PRIDE: Yes. Me again.
BARRY: What do you want this time?
PRIDE: I've just got a few questions.
BARRY: All right.
PRIDE: Shall we go outside?
BARRY: OK. But please make it quick. As soon as I've finished working on that plane, I've got to give Sarah's plane a service.
PRIDE: Oh, really? Is she going to use it?
BARRY: Yes. She wants to get away, she says. She's going to fly off tomorrow morning.
PRIDE: Oh, is she? Now then, Barry, when did you last see Rose?

. . . .

BRIAN: But this company was Robert's. He wanted you to have it.
SARAH: Yes, but I don't want it. First Robert dies, now Rose has been killed.
BRIAN: What are you talking about?
SARAH: Well, the Inspector thinks she was murdered, doesn't she?
BRIAN: But who — Everybody likes Rose.
SARAH: Do they? What about Barry?
BRIAN: What about Barry? Sarah you don't think Barry. . .
SARAH: I don't know. I hope Inspector Wade has discovered the murderer's identity.
BRIAN: Well, I don't believe any of it. But anyway, Sarah, about Cutter's Air Taxis, about the company. I won't allow you to sell it.
SARAH: You can't stop me.
BRIAN: Oh yes, I can. I certainly can.

. . . .

SARAH: Hello, Inspector. Good morning, Sergeant Pride.
WADE: Good morning, Mrs Cutter.
BRIAN: What do you want, Inspector?
WADE: Mrs Cutter, if a pilot is going to crash, does he open the door of the plane?
SARAH: No.
WADE: Why not?
SARAH: Because he's trying to control the aircraft. But he might open the door if . . .
WADE: If what, Mrs Cutter?
SARAH: If he is going to parachute out of the plane.
BRIAN: Look, Inspector, what is this all about?
WADE: Shall we all sit down?
SARAH: Why?
PRIDE: Just do what the Inspector says, please.
BRIAN: What's going to happen?
WADE: We're going to wait.
SARAH: Wait for what, Inspector?
WADE: Not what, Mrs Cutter, who. We're going to wait for the person who would like to kill you!

Unit 18

ANNOUNCER: The Air Taxi Mystery.

ANNOUNCER: Part 9. The Solution.

BRIAN: Look, Inspector, how long are we going to wait?

WADE: Don't worry, Mr Neal. It won't be long now.

SARAH: But who is it, Inspector? Who wants to kill me?

WADE: You'll soon see, Mrs Cutter.

BRIAN: Well, I think this is ridiculous.

SARAH: Listen!

BRIAN: Glenda!

GLENDA: Sarah. Are you going to sell the company? You can't you know, and Brian won't let you. I'll make him. Oh. . . Inspector. Hello. What a lot of people! What's going on? Why are you all here?

WADE: Glenda Neal, I arrest you for the murders of Robert Cutter and Rose Melville.

PRIDE: You do not have to say anything, but anything you say will be taken down and may be used in evidence.

GLENDA: But there's been a mistake. You can't be serious! Robert and Rose died in air accidents.

PRIDE: They weren't accidents, Mrs Neal, and you know it.

BRIAN: What the hell are you talking about?

WADE: Two clever murders! Your wife used the same method each time. She hid in the aeroplane before take off, killed the pilot, set the controls, and then she sent an SOS message before she parachuted to safety — out of the door.

BRIAN: But why? Why would Glenda want to do that?

GLENDA: You always were stupid, Brian.

WADE: When Robert Cutter died, his wife, Sarah, inherited the company.

SARAH: That's right. I did.

WADE: If Sarah dies, who gets Cutter Air Taxis?

BRIAN: I haven't really thought about it. Umm. I'm Sarah's brother, and she doesn't have any other relations, so. . . er. . . me!

WADE: Exactly! The company would be yours — and that means Glenda's, of course.

SARAH: Poor Brian. Glenda has always controlled you, hasn't she?

BRIAN: But. . . but Sarah's still alive.

WADE: Yes. She's very lucky. She was next on the list.

SARAH: Why did Rose have to die?

PRIDE: Rose was working on her aeroplane one evening. She heard Glenda talking to Barry about Robert Cutter's murder, so she had to die.

SARAH: Wait a minute, Sergeant. Barry?

PRIDE: Yes.

GLENDA: Barry had nothing to do with it!

WADE: No, but he knew all about the murders, didn't he?

GLENDA: All right. All right. I love him and he loves me. I told him everything. I thought — but it's too late now!

BRIAN: Glenda, how could you?

WADE: Sergeant Pride.

PRIDE: Inspector?

WADE: Take her away.

....

TONY: Oh Sheila, it is nice to be in Cornwall again.

WADE: Yes, and this time I hope an aeroplane won't crash into our field.

TONY: I hope not. How did you know it was murder, Sheila? When did you suspect?

WADE: Immediately. I thought — why was the plane's door open? Then there was the seventeen minutes between the SOS message and the crash. And then I realised that Rose's death was the same as Robert Cutter's — and then I saw Glenda Neal's parachuting trophy!

TONY: Listen.

WADE: What's the matter love?

TONY: What's that noise? It's not another aeroplane, is it?

WADE: Relax! It's only the farmer on his tractor. Shall I make us a coffee?

Grammar summary

(Note: these do not always follow the order of the units.)

PRESENT PERFECT

Have you ever	had a terrible nightmare? seen an accident?	Yes, I have. No, I haven't.

I You We They	have	always	danced for fun. played for local teams.
He She It	has		

It's the	noisiest party	they've	ever	had.
	dirtiest room	she's		seen.
	most interesting book	he's		read.

He She	has	just	won a gold medal. got married. spent too much money.
I You We They	have		

How long have you	been a student? lived in this house? worn glasses?	Since	1986. last December.
		For	six months. a year.

I/You/We/They	have	not	watched TV written a letter	since Tuesday. for six months.
He/She	has			

DIRECTIONS/INSTRUCTIONS

Can you tell me how to	get to the cinema? use this camera?

Take the	first second	turning on the	left. right.	It's on your	left. right.

First Then	look through the viewfinder press the button	and	focus the lens. wind on the film.

DISTANCES AND LOCATION

How far is it from	Bechar Boston	to	Adrar? New York?

Where is	Bechar? Boston?	It's	south-east north-east	of	Fes. New York.

TOO AND ENOUGH

There is	too much not enough	light. snow.

There are	too many not enough	people. chairs.

He is	too weak not strong enough	to	lift the suitcase. unscrew the bottletop.

PASSIVES

I/He/She/It	was	rescued injured	(by the police). (by a wave).
We/You/They	were		

I/You/We/They	have	(just) been	knocked down. arrested.
He/She	has		

DESCRIPTIONS

It	looks smells tastes	horrible. fantastic. delicious. revolting.	
They	look smell taste	very quite rather	expensive. uncomfortable. young. poor.

HOPE

I hope you	had a good time. are going to visit us. are feeling well.

COMPARISONS

Which is	bigger, older, more expensive,	Juno or Neptune?

Who is the	strongest oldest tallest youngest		person at the circus?
	most	beautiful handsome	

The Palace Hotel The Sea View Hotel	is	more	expensive comfortable	than	the Sea View Hotel.
		cleaner			
	is not as	old-fashioned modern uncomfortable		as	the Palace Hotel.

REPORTED SPEECH

He The woman They	told asked	him the man them	to	clean the car. stop talking. leave the room.

PAST CONTINUOUS

What	was	I/he/she/it	doing	when	the tent collapsed? the telephone rang?	I/He/She/It	was	having a bath. watching TV.
	were	you/we/they				You/We/They	were	

OBLIGATION

I/You/We/They	must have to	wear a suit. carry a pass. keep quiet.
He/She/It	must has to	

I/You/We/They	do not	have to	get up early. wear a uniform.
He/She/It	does not		

It means that you must not	smoke. walk on the grass. take photographs.

CONDITIONALS TYPE 1

General

If	the car breaks down, you are trapped in the lift,	you should	call the garage. press the red button.

Future

If	it rains, there are any problems,	she will	go to the theatre. call for help.

TIME CLAUSES

Before After As soon as	I/you/he/she/we/they	arrive(s),	I/you/he/she/we/they	will start playing. will telephone you.

What happened while	he was they were	cooking?

What did	he they	do	as soon as when	he heard the alarm? they got home?

While	he was they were	talking	a friend called.

KNOW/THINK/HOPE

She	knows thinks hopes	he will (probably)	take three hours. win the prize. reach the top.

FUTURE PROBABILITY

What will	I/you/he/she/we/they	be doing	at ten o'clock? in two weeks? on Monday morning?

I/You/He/She/We/They	will (probably)	be	visiting Florence. watching TV. talking to the doctor.

List of irregular verbs

Verbs with an asterisk (*) against them occurred in *Meridian Plus Student's Book 1*.

infinitive	past simple	past participle
be*	was/were	been
begin	began	begun
break	broke	broken
bring	brought	brought
burn	burned/burnt	burned/burnt
buy*	bought	bought
can	could	—
catch*	caught	caught
choose	chose	chosen
come*	came	come
cut	cut	cut
do*	did	done
drink	drank	drunk
drive*	drove	driven
eat*	ate	eaten
fall*	fell	fallen
feed	fed	fed
feel*	felt	felt
find*	found	found
fly*	flew	flown
forget*	forgot	forgotten
get*	got	got
give*	gave	given
go*	went	been/gone
have*	had	had
hear*	heard	heard
hit	hit	hit
hurt	hurt	hurt
keep	kept	kept
know*	knew	known
lay	laid	laid
learn	learned/ learnt	learned/learnt
leave*	left	left
let*	let	let
lie*	lay	lain
lose	lost	lost
make*	made	made
mean	meant	meant
meet*	met	met
oversleep*	overslept	overslept
pay*	paid	paid
put*	put	put
read*	read	read
ride*	rode	ridden
ring*	rang	rung
run	ran	run
say*	said	said
see*	saw	seen
sell*	sold	sold
send	sent	sent
set	set	set
show	showed	shown
sing*	sang	sung
sit*	sat	sat
sleep*	slept	slept
smell*	smelled/smelt	smelled/smelt
speak*	spoke	spoken
spend*	spent	spent
spill	spilled/spilt	spilled/spilt
stand	stood	stood
steal	stole	stolen
swim*	swam	swum
swing	swung	swung
take*	took	taken

infinitive	past simple	past participle
teach*	taught	taught
tear	tore	torn
tell*	told	told
think*	thought	thought
throw*	threw	thrown
wake up*	woke up	woken up
wear*	wore	worn
win*	won	won
wind on	wound on	wound on
write*	wrote	written

Wordlist

1 This wordlist gives the unit number and page of the Student's Book where the item first occurs (e.g. 7:28 = Unit 7, page 28).
2 All verbs are listed in the infinitive. Past forms of the verb are not included. (See List of irregular verbs, page 120.)
3 The list does not include vocabulary from the Reading texts on the fourth page of each unit, but it does include vocabulary from the questions on these texts.
4 The list does not include vocabulary from the Classwork and Listening activities.
5 The following abbreviations are used: *n* (noun); *v* (verb); *adj* (adjective); *adv* (adverb); *prep* (preposition); *aux v* (auxiliary verb).
6 Words with an asterisk (*) against them occurred in Student's Book 1.

Longman Group UK Limited,
Longman House, Burnt Mill, Harlow,
Essex CM20 2JE, England
and Associated Companies throughout the world.

© Longman Group UK Limited 1988
All rights reserved; no part of this publication may be reproduced, stored in a retrieval system, or transmitted in any form or by any means, electronic, mechanical, photocopying, recording, or otherwise, without the prior written permission of the Publishers.

First published 1988
Third Impression 1989
Fourth Impression 1989

ISBN 0-582-02746-2

Set in 10/12pt Linotron 202 Century Schoolbook
Printed in Italy
by G. Canale & C. S.p.A. Turin

Illustrated by Andrew Aloof, Robin Edmunds, Tony Kenyon, Eric Robson (The Garden Studio), David Parkins, Ray Burrows, Louis MacKay, Ed Mclachlan

Acknowledgements
We are grateful to the following for permission to reproduce copyright photographs:

Airviews (Manchester) Limited for page 23 (bottom); Ann Kendall/Cusichaca Project for page 31 (bottom); BBC Copyright/Ann Kendall for page 31 (top); BBC Copyright/Tom Baker and Terence Rigby for page 61 (left); Bruce Coleman Limited for page 35 (bottom); Camera 1 for page 22 (bottom left); Camera Press Limited for pages 19 and 62 (top); The J Allan Cash Photolibrary for page 43 (top); Castaway by Lucy Irvine/Victor Gollancz Limited (Gary Steer) for page 47; Central Electricity Generating Board for page 23 (top); Daily Mirror for page 67 (bottom); Feature-Pix for page 33; Impact Photos/Alain Le Garsmeur for page 51; Julia Hunt Model Agency for page 39; London Express News and Feature Service for page 27 (top); London Features International Limited for page 22 (top); London Regional Transport Underground Map, registered users no. 85/461; Longman Photographic Unit for pages 13,16,29,55 and 62 (bottom); National Film Archive/Paramount Pictures Corporation for pages 7 (bottom), 22 (bottom right) and 61 (top right); National Film Archive/ Orion Pictures International for page 7 (top); National Film Archive/Walt Disney Productions for page 61 (right); The Photo Source Limited for page 64; Picturepoint-London for pages 4,11,28 and 35 (top); Scope Features/ Brian Moody for page 15; The Sun for page 67 (middle); Topham Picture Library for pages 48 and 67 (top); Westfalisches Amt fur Denkmalpflege for page 63; Zefa Picture Library (UK) Limited for pages 43 (bottom) and 55 (right)

Aprobado por el Ministerio de Educación y Ciencia
con fecha 22 de junio de 1988.